Embracing the Journey

LEARNING TO GROW WHEN LIFE DOESN'T
WORK OUT AS PLANNED

Embracing the Journey

LEARNING TO GROW WHEN LIFE DOESN'T WORK OUT AS PLANNED

BY SARAH STYF

Book Cover by Matt Holman

First edition 2023

To Jeff, L, and E: embracing life's journey is a daily choice made easier because you are doing it with me. I love all three of you so very much.

Contents

Introduction

Writing It Down

I STARTED BLOGGING SHORTLY after I started graduate school.

It wasn't like I had a lot of time. I was teaching and going to class and parenting a baby and a toddler. But my husband Jeff and I had bought a fixer-upper that we had already started renovating.

We were two years into making big changes and I discovered I was well behind blogging as a communication medium.

When our family moved from Fort Wayne to Texas, I dropped my *Frazzled Reflections* blog on Blogger and moved to a more sophisticated WordPress account. The new blog became a dumping ground for all of my thoughts, concerns, fears, and triumphs. In the seven years since I started that second blog and then moved it to another platform, I have written about faith, family, travel, and politics. While I sometimes deviate from the original intent to talk about the "unexpected journey," I keep coming back to it because it is the theme of my life.

My most consistently popular writings have been my many posts about camping and our family travel adventures, and that is to be expected. After all, in the algorithms of internet writing, the people make clear what they want: posts that tell them about the places they want to travel to.

But writing has always been my go-to for processing the realities of life, and my blog has always been where I could do that publicly. Even when I was writing about camping with my family, the pieces that mattered the most to me were the ones where I dug into my soul and got honest, first with myself, and then with anyone willing to listen.

I eventually realized that with over 300 blog posts from nearly a decade of writing on the internet, I might actually have enough to put a select few related pieces into a single book of essays reflecting on "the journey."

I wanted a collection of my writing that would show the evolution of a woman who is so many things: wife, mother, teacher, sister, and friend. I wanted to capture my growth over the seven-year period after we moved to Texas, a period of my life when I finally learned what it was to be *me*.

I learned to listen to the work instead of making the work become what I wanted it to be. I surprised myself as I read words I hadn't considered in years, particularly regarding our move from Fort Wayne to Houston. I realized just how much of the emotional journey repeated itself six years later, even though the reasons for moving and our family's overall response were so different from what they had been when we were younger, fresher, and slightly more naïve. So much would happen over the six years that we lived in Texas, both to us and to our country, that I marveled at how much of what I wrote still held true for me. The revision process wasn't just about making the original better or truer to who I am today; it took me on a journey through the past to where I am now.

While I touch on how my life was impacted by living through a global pandemic, I left most of those reflections for another time and space. Those words were meant for the moments in which they were written. While I touch on my faith and politics, two issues that have gotten occasional time on all of my blogs over the past decade, I also leave most of my reflections on my journey of faith and political beliefs for another time and, hopefully, another book.

This book is about growing up into middle age. It's about finding a place to belong over and over again. It's about figuring out what kind of mother I want to be and the dreams I have for my children. And it's about finding healing when it feels like I was broken beyond repair.

Thank you for joining me on this journey. I hope you will see a little of yourself learning to accept and embrace a journey often out of our individual control.

Growth

A Life of Unexpected

No one's life is predictable. It seems like an obvious statement, but one that so many of us struggle to accept. The unpredictable meets us before we're born and follows us our entire lives. The unpredictable can destroy and enrich, bring hurt and healing, and form us in ways we don't fully understand until years after the fact.

I'm sure that my mom never expected to have her first baby thousands of miles away from her Michigan family when she gave birth to me on a hot June day in southern California. When my dad got a new position at a Detroit area high school, she eagerly returned to her home state with a toddler on her lap. We lived for the next eight years in that little bungalow in Detroit proper, where my parents welcomed two of my three little sisters. After eight years growing up a city kid, nine-year-old me never expected to move from the Motor City to a much smaller town in Illinois. Two years later we moved to the "middle-of-nowhere" Wyoming, this time with my third baby sister, an infant asleep in a car seat, oblivious to the upheaval in our family's life. I exchanged my expectations of spending my sixth-grade year playing basketball and cheerleading alongside my friends for navigating the world of middle school mean-girl politics without the support I desperately needed.

Five years later, I found out I had achieved my two-year goal of making it into the elite jazz choir at my high school. The next day my dad received word that he had been offered a position to serve at a school and church in southwest Michigan, far away from my Wyoming friends, youth group, and choir. The day after my sixteenth birthday he told me he had accepted the position. Instead of spending my junior year singing in jazz choir and enjoying all of the junior year festivities with my friends, I started over at a new high school with new politics and new expectations.

Determined to hate everything about our family's move, I spent the next two years planning for my college future. I was going to meet a perfect Lutheran boy at my small Lutheran college in Nebraska. We would graduate, get married, and begin our perfect lives serving at a church that wanted us. I would teach for a couple of years and then we would raise perfect Lutheran babies while I stayed home with them.

Instead, less than a week after we both graduated from the same high school, I met my Dutch, Christian Reformed future husband in the parking lot of the McDonald's where I worked. Instead of having babies within a couple of years of teaching, I discovered I really *loved* teaching and I didn't want to leave the classroom. When we were finally ready to have babies, my body didn't cooperate, and instead of seeing the words "Pregnant" on home test after test, we kept getting negative results. The month we were told that we weren't going to get pregnant and we were going to have to try something different, my body decided to cooperate and I got pregnant.

I planned to raise our new daughter in Indianapolis. Instead, the day after my 30th birthday, my husband Jeff came home and told me he was getting transferred to Fort Wayne in the next year. I had no desire to leave a place I loved where we had friends who had become family, but our limited choices meant one more unexpected change.

In the first years we lived in Fort Wayne, I started and completed grad school. I taught college for the first time. We had another surprise baby. I got a job at the high school where I wanted to teach with less than two weeks to prepare before the school year started. I started teaching AP Language. We watched our house go through many changes. I cried. I laughed. I cried. I loved. I learned. I cried some more. At times it felt like we were in a free fall with no soft landing in sight. Other times we were slowly climbing up the next hill, only to tumble down the other side once we crested the top. And all along the journey we grew as a family (both physically and metaphorically), we grew professionally, and we made close work friendships that remain many years later.

All of those unexpected changes prepared us for a step beyond our wildest dreams: we moved to Texas.

God has a funny sense of humor. After five years living in Wyoming in my youth, I was convinced I would return to the West as an adult. I would someday live in Colorado, close to the desert and mountains. Instead, this desert-loving, mountain-hiking, freshwater Lake Michiganadoring Midwesterner moved her family to wet, humid southeastern Texas close to the salty Gulf of Mexico.

Six years later, after adventures and lessons that we could only learn from living in the Lone Star State, we returned to Indiana. Bruised and battered and in serious need of the healing that could only come with a return to the familiar, we left behind the life that we thought we wanted for a life that finally felt like home.

My life has been a series of unexpected events. People say, "Man plans and God laughs." I still haven't learned. I haven't learned to stop planning every part of my life. I haven't learned to let go of what I believe should be. I haven't learned to let go of what could have been.

But God keeps giving me the opportunity to learn to accept and embrace the unexpected.

Running

I AM NOT AN athlete.

In my early adolescence I did play softball (I wasn't great) and basketball (I wasn't awful).

But for my freshman and sophomore years I participated in track. Even saying I "participated" is a little generous. I am not fast, I have no upper body strength, and I have short legs. My high school biology teacher tried to convince me to try distance running, but I refused. After all, who would want to run several miles a day? It sounded awful. But I wanted to be on the track team so I decided to sign up for long jump.

Once again, I've always been slow and I have short legs. I was the LAST person who should have been attempting the long jump. Yet for two years I went to daily practices and ran and jumped with teammates who were significantly faster and stronger than me. I ran ladders, sprints, a couple two-mile runs, and learned just how hard a high school athlete has to work. I placed last in every practice and every meet. I even remember missing my event in one meet because I didn't hear the long jump announcement.

I also spent the better part of my sophomore season suffering from painful shin splints. I iced my legs every night and endured through the remainder of the season. I'm sure it was a combination of issues: improper technique, poor running shoes, a body not designed for sprinting. When my family moved to Michigan and I moved to a new high school, I swore off of running forever. It was painful, and I was slow. If I was going to exercise I would find other methods to stay in shape.

For much of my adult life, my sporadic exercise habits usually centered on my access to workout equipment. In college, I lost the Freshman 15 on a Stairmaster. After marriage, I used the local YMCA whenever we had an active membership. Then we moved to Texas and to an area where we didn't have easy access to a YMCA. The pre-move stress, the six weeks living in our camper, and the time spent adjusting to a new city added on pounds I had proudly lost a year after our son's birth. I needed to make a change and it needed to be both affordable and accessible. That is when my husband suggested I start running.

It was laughable. After all, I had learned to hate running as a teenager, and at the time of this "helpful" suggestions from my husband, I was closer to 40 than 30. If running had been hard on my body when I was 15, what would it do to my thirty-something body? But I had to do something and running meant all I had to do was put on my New Balance shoes and walk out of our front door.

I downloaded a running app and started running. In the beginning it wasn't so terrible. When I only had to run nine out of thirty minutes, my body wasn't screaming at me to stop. But the runs got longer and the walks shorter. It took me about twelve weeks instead of the prescribed eight weeks and eventually I ran three miles without the prompted assistance of the app. Shin splints? Not at all. In fact, after seven years of running now, I mostly deal with muscle aches when I don't take the time to stretch once I'm done.

I guess I should have listened to my biology teacher all those years ago.[1] Now my weeks don't feel complete if I don't run. My body starts to twitch and beg to move. After learning to run in the heat and humidity, I'm now learning to embrace running in the cold. It's not just about my health. It's also the lesson I'm

---

1. In fact, a friend convinced me to run the 2016 Final Four Four-Mile race in Houston shortly after I reached my three-mile goal. Knowing that I could run four miles without great difficulty convinced me to keep routine, even on the hottest Houston days.

teaching my children—taking care of yourself is about finding the right physical activity for you.

I never expected to embrace running as my physical activity of choice, but now I can't imagine doing anything else.

Kitchen Lessons

My STAY-AT-HOME MOM COOKED and baked all the time. My parents carefully managed every penny, so we couldn't resort to eating out when she was too tired to cook or the week was too busy. Like most kids, there were dishes that I never learned to appreciate, meals that I've never been able to bring myself to eat again as an adult (it took years before I was willing to try new and improved recipes for preparing fish), but I also had my favorites. My neighborhood childhood friends still mention their love for my mom's homemade bread, fresh out of the oven, and every Christmas I wistfully recall tin after tin of cookies safely stored in the pantry.

But even with a mom who cooked all of the time, I spent little time during my childhood learning how to cook and bake. I occasionally helped my mom in the kitchen, and there were a few times where she needed my help. I tried to stir the flour into the wet ingredients to create bread dough, and then usually gave up when it got too hard to mix the ingredients, refusing to learn how to properly kneed the unfinished dough. My mom put me in charge of stirring the filling for fresh fruit pie, but I impatiently waited for the gel filling to clear, barely avoiding the smell of burned sugar. I loved eating my mom's homemade mac and cheese, but I could rarely be trusted to *not* let the roux burn on the stove. Looking back, I'm not sure if it was a lack of desire or a lack of training that kept me out of the kitchen. By the time I turned eighteen, I had spent more time in front of a play kitchen than in the actual kitchen.

As a result, in my twenties I accepted my fate as a notoriously bad cook. Looking back, it wasn't that I was a terrible cook, I was just woefully lacking in knowledge and practice, bumbling along whenever I was forced to do things for myself. My freshman year of high school I exploded a pot of boiling water in my Foods and Nutrition class because I didn't know the difference between a clear cooking pot and a casserole dish. When my mom was visiting my ill grandmother, I nearly ruined a pan of enchiladas after spilling an entire can of enchilada sauce on the counter. My senior year of high school I burned my foot with hot pasta water as I carried it from the stove to the sink. After I moved into my first apartment with my college roommates, the best cooking we did consisted of chicken on a George Foreman Grill. Shortly after getting married I misread the directions (making mistakes with cup measurements) and added too much water to a "just add water" boxed meal; we ended up with soup instead of biscuits.

When I got my first teaching job, I was working in Illinois, Jeff was working in Michigan (in a different time zone), and we were living in Indiana. Between our work hours and commutes, I didn't have much time to teach myself how to be a quality cook. I made half-hearted attempts on the nights we were both home and I had enough energy, the bulk of my quality cooking taking place in a crockpot because it required few ingredients and little preparation. Looking back, I could probably count the number of times I used the oven in our first house on my hands.

Then we moved to Indianapolis. We were living and working in the same city, we lived less than five minutes from the school where I was teaching, and we started getting a little more adventurous. We bought a new grill and then an electric smoker, and we learned how to diversify both our indoor and outdoor cooking. Thankfully, I eventually learned how to cook something besides Hamburger Helper, but the process was slow and sometimes painful to the senses. The trial and error became necessary as we also learned to love hosting friends and family, sharing the Thanksgiving and Easter dinner duties with our close group of friends, determined to outdo what we had prepared the year before.

Parenthood and our move to Fort Wayne made home cooking a necessity. During our first year in our new home, I was in graduate school, we primarily depended on one salary, and our fixer-upper was falling apart around us. It didn't matter how busy we were or how exhausted I might be from school or pregnancy, we just didn't have the money to resort to take-out two to three times a week. We had to eat at home, and I had to make the money stretch as far as I could.

I learned how to look for different recipes and try new spices. Once I gained some confidence, I discovered that I loved the creative process of cooking. When I mastered one skill I could move on to the next, adjusting recipes to match our taste preferences. Jeff started mixing our own meat rubs, the result of hours spent looking for new barbecuing recipes and methods. Cooking together increased our marital communication and brought us together in new ways. Kitchen collaboration redefined sexy in our home. After all, when we were in college he wooed me with cheesecake that he made himself, a skill he continues to use to impress friends, family, and coworkers.

When I was a kid, I begged my parents to take us out to eat, something that adulthood has taught me was quite the sacrifice for our family of six. But I consider it a compliment that our kids often beg to stay home. They have their favorites and they make specific requests, but it is rare that they don't like something we have put on the table. Their desire for home cooking has forced me to ditch the boxed lasagna for homemade and cake made from scratch as opposed to a mix. We've allowed them to slowly learn how to make their own easy meals, starting with boxed mac and cheese and moving to barbecue sauces and baked goods.

Oh, we have days and weeks when the act of meal preparation is more work than I can face. When the schedules overlap or we've had an exhausting week, suddenly pizza from our favorite local place or Chinese take-out sounds like a lifeline more than a surrender. Yet even during those weeks, I hesitate to hand over the grocery shopping to my willing husband. While I may normally hate shopping, I love picking out the ingredients for the following week of meals, planning as I look for sales and the best-looking available fresh food.

I've stopped seeing my kitchen as a place where my working mom homemaking skills go to die. Instead, it is a place where I can cook healthy meals for my family, bond with my husband, or teach my children skills that will help them through college and beyond. It's a place where we test the pulled pork fresh off of the smoker or eat the leftover pieces of baked pie crust that I cut off of the chicken pot pie baking in the oven.

I just keep dreaming about creating a gourmet kitchen to match.

On Turning 40

I CLEARLY REMEMBER MY dad's fortieth birthday. We were on a family spring break vacation, driving from Wyoming to Oregon to visit my aunt and uncle and new baby cousin. We had stayed in a motel overnight, and while we were packing up for the second day of our trip, my dad somehow managed to throw a shoe onto the roof of the roadside motel. While it doesn't come up often, we haven't let him forget that he spent part of his fortieth birthday trying to figure out how to get a shoe off of a roof.

I remember when I used to be excited about birthdays. Those milestones meant new privileges and responsibilities. And then the milestones just meant that I was one year older, something I didn't necessarily look forward to.

Thirty was rough. I really didn't want to leave my twenties behind. Our daughter was born just six weeks before my thirtieth birthday and I relentlessly teased Jeff because I became a parent before I turned thirty and he didn't. Thirty sounded old, like I suddenly needed to act like a responsible adult. And it wasn't that I didn't *already* act like a responsible adult. I was married and a high school teacher with little free time. When we did get together with our friends, we didn't go to bars or clubs; instead we hung out at each other's houses (houses that we all owned), talked, played games, and drank (mostly) responsibly. But something about the combination of motherhood and my thirtieth birthday put me into a little bit of a funk.

Jeff surprised me with a party of our closest friends on my actual birthday, and I started to dream about all the things my thirties could mean. The next day he dropped the bomb that his boss wanted to transfer him to a new city; suddenly the hopes I had drawn up for the next decade of my life were blown to smithereens.

But life is a series of highs and lows and no decade of our life is going to be a trouble-free journey across a wide, open plain. My 30s brought me a second baby, a graduate degree, three different jobs, two moves, two new dogs, a long winding road to financial stability, a new discovery of health when I lost all the baby weight and then some (and humility when I gained back the "and then some"), on a regular basis once I was in the second half of the decade, new adventures with my family when, and the rediscovery of my love for writing. My thirties weren't perfect, but as I neared the end of the decade, I looked back at everything I learned and experienced and realized ten years later I was stronger and ready to face new unknowns.

Where thirty felt like the end of something, forty felt like the beginning.

I used to think that the number forty was so old, like once I hit forty years of life, it would be the end of everything good. That "over the hill" meant I didn't have more to look forward to. Instead, on my fortieth birthday I looked towards the future and saw another decade of potential highs and lows and learning and growth, and I couldn't wait to see where it took me.

Shortly before I turned forty I listened to an episode of Jen Hatmaker's *For the Love* podcast during which she spoke to Rich Karlgaard from.[1] As a mom and a teacher, I was convicted by his discussion of the pressure that kids are feeling to do it all and be it all so early in their lives. But I was also encouraged by the idea that life isn't over at forty or fifty. Dreams are still possible. New goals are still achievable. I can continue to grow and evolve as a woman, wife, mother, and professional. I hadn't peaked, and there was no reason to feel like I *should* have already.

---

1. "It's Okay to Be a Late Bloomer: Forbes Magazine's Rich Karlgaard." *For the Love Podcast*, created by Jen Hatmaker, season 17, episode 5, 4 June 2019

As I looked to my fortieth birthday, I started writing a list of goals for the next year, and then I realized that my life had changed so much in the previous ten, how could I possibly know what the next ten would hold? I was not the exact same person at forty as I was when I turned thirty. How could I box myself into arbitrary goals that seemed like a good idea at the time but didn't fit my life as it changed? As I faced the curveballs that send life off of the planned track? As my family continued to grow and change in ways both imagined and unimagined?

What did I want my forties to look like?

I wanted to pursue health and healthy body image over a number on a scale. When I started running, I thought I was pretty fit. I wasn't wrong, and while my fitness level has fluctuated much since I first laced up my running shoes, I at least continue to try to be consistent. But I also decided that life is too short to deny myself the pleasures of good food, an occasional glass of wine or a margarita, or my favorite snack—buttered movie theater popcorn.

I wanted to be more intentional about making and maintaining my friendships. My 30s started with fantastically close friendships in a friend circle that drifted after we moved to a new city. We all had babies and jobs and we were moving farther apart geographically. Those friendships still remain, and we made good friends when we moved to Houston, but my introverted self finds it far easier to stay in my own bubble than to reach out of my comfort zone to extend new hands of friendship. But I see the importance and value of close female friendships. My husband may truly be my best friend, but I still need my girlfriends who understand the unique challenges of being a woman, wife, mother, and daughter.

I wanted to be the change I want to see in the world. I wanted to be more ecologically and environmentally responsible, smarter and more generous with my resources, less wasteful of the things I have and more focused on my needs than on-the-whim wants, and seek to find solutions instead of just complaining about the problems. I wanted to be an example that my children and students can follow, so they can see what it is to both say they are Christians and *be* Christians. I wanted to serve Jesus by serving others. I had no idea what that looked like, but I believed it was never too late to start trying to find out.

I wanted to pursue dreams and accept the challenges that go with those dreams. I'm not old. God willing, I have a lot of time left, but I didn't want to just keep saying "next year." The untimely death of Christian writer Rachel Held Evans shortly before I turned forty reminded me that every day is a gift and that I needed to use the time that God has given me. Sometimes we need to say "not yet," but our lives shouldn't be a list of "somedays." I kept writing. I continued to travel. I wouldn't just dream about returning to Europe, but I would find a way to use the passport that we got a few years after moving to Texas so that we could spend a few hours in Mexico.[2] I didn't believe God was done with me.

I wanted to be better about focusing on my family. I can be a hopeless workaholic, and because I both love what I do and I am a relentless people-pleaser, I often find myself sacrificing for my job over my family. I know that there is no such thing as a perfect balance, but I wanted to find true satisfaction in my job as both mother and teacher without losing myself at the same time. I didn't want to stop reading and writing and bettering myself as a wife, mom, teacher, and citizen, but I also needed to take the time to just *be* a wife, mom, teacher, and productive citizen.

I had no idea that my dreams for my forties would face challenges less than a year later as a global pandemic brought the world to a stop. I had no idea that a year and a half later I would face a career crisis that would challenge my faith and cause me to question everything I had ever believed about myself. I had no idea that my forty-second birthday would coincide with a drastic

---

2. Instead of Europe, Jeff and I celebrated our twentieth wedding anniversary a few months late when we went to Hawaii during my spring break. While I do want to go back to Europe someday, that trip was more than I could have imagined.

decision to turn our family's life upside down by returning to Indiana.

Reading Shauna Niequist's book *I Guess I Haven't Learned That Yet* felt like a window into my own life experiences. She writes:

> The first part of my forties has been an unwinding of the threads that wrapped around my life, a throwing off of all the lines, a systematic and painful series of unbelongings…It was…someone peeling my fingers, one by one, away from the life I'd been clutching with white knuckles, the life that didn't fit anymore, no matter how hard I was trying to hold on.[3]

My forties haven't exactly gone the way I planned, but that's the theme of my life. However, I like who I am in my forties. My life may have gotten messier than I anticipated, but the person I am now just might be the most authentic version of myself I've ever been.

And I feel that deserves celebration.

---

3. Shauna Niequist, *I Guess I Haven't Learned That Yet*, p. 63

A Letter to Me

MANY OF US CAN point to specific formative moments in our adolescence, moments that made us the people we are today.

So often we focus on the negative because it's easy to see the negative while in the midst of struggle. It's hard to forget the events that keep us awake at night. When we do bury them, they often come back to haunt us.

But the positive moments in life also shape us. They too form us into the people we become.

That is why I will never forget the impact of studying abroad my junior year of college. This is what I would tell myself, if I could.

Dear 20-year-old Me,

You are about to embark on the journey of a lifetime. After months of convincing Mom and Dad that this is a good idea, planning out everything you want to see and do, and working every shift possible during the summer, you are ready. You think you know the impact this will have on your life, but take comfort in knowing that you don't know anything, and that will make the next three months so much better. This journey will change you and set you on a path that is even better than the life you are imagining for yourself right now, the memories and the lessons sticking with you long after you return to the States.

What will the next three and a half months look like?

You'll walk around Paris and write on a bench outside of Notre Dame, dreaming of a return trip in the next three months. Nineteen years later you'll regret that this return trip never happened as you watch the centuries-old cathedral burn on international news. You'll mourn the potential loss of history and place of worship for all who travel through the city but be inspired by the resilience of the French people as they make plans to rebuild.

You'll tour ancient Roman ruins while walking miles in the rain and discover the Spanish Steps three times in a single night when you and your traveling companions walk in circles trying to find the hostel where you left your luggage. And while you will be irritable and exhausted, you'll crash into bed satisfied that you have walked in the footsteps of historical giants.

You will inadvertently show up at the Vatican on the same day that Pope John Paul II is giving a sermon on the steps of St. Peter's, at first confused by the large number of people but then zooming in your camera as much as possible for a glimpse of the man who drew a large crowd of the faithful. While you will hear words over the loudspeaker, you will not understand the Italian being spoken, but your Lutheran heart will revel in the fact that you were in the same general space as the Holy Father.

You will walk for what seems like miles through every hall of the Vatican Museum, taking in artifacts that go back centuries while eagerly looking for the signs that repeatedly say "Sistine Chapel this way." Even though it has been your dream throughout adolescence, you will be underwhelmed by the size of the small room showcasing Michelangelo's masterpiece (because for some reason you never considered that the word "chapel" might actually refer to a chapel). And twenty years later you will still feel guilty that it wasn't a highlight of your trip.

You'll feel the very real presence of God while standing in the middle of a magnificent structure paid for with indulgences and months later grieve the commonplace emptiness of grand European cathedrals on Sunday mornings.

You'll be shocked by the size of Michelangelo's David and moved by the beauty of Florence's streets and cathedrals.

You'll be forever changed by the grounds of Dachau and dedicate your future career to teaching your students about oppression and injustice.

You'll be rescued from being thrown off of a train by an Italian in a gay pride t-shirt, pointed to the correct Munich train by two fellow college-aged Texan Mormons on their two-year mission, and wake up one morning with a stranger sleeping in the fourth bed in a semi-sketchy hostel in Paris.

You'll discover just how difficult it was for "groundlings" to stand through an entire Shakespeare performance and then sob through the second act of Miss Saigon, PMS amplifying the fact that you desperately miss a boyfriend that only a month before you had considered breaking up with.

You'll listen as your visiting professor preaches endlessly about Edward de Vere, the 17th Earl of Oxford, and be the only one of your classmates who refuses to believe that Will Shakespeare wasn't the real author of his plays. And then you'll regret your decision to not go to Stratford-upon-Avon by yourself and be reminded of that decision every single time you teach a Shakespeare play to your future students.

You'll fall in love with Edinburgh and spend the rest of your life correcting people who mispronounce the name of one of the most beautiful cities you have ever visited.

While you've always said you love nature, you will develop a lifelong love for the outdoors as you hike in the rain through Killarney National Park. After being in Killarney for only a couple days, another tourist will stop you to ask for directions, boosting your confidence that you actually look like you know what you're doing after two months of traveling abroad. The green hills, salty coastline, and friendly locals will embed the Emerald Isle into your heart and you'll long for the day you will someday return, which still hasn't happened yet.

You'll grow in independence as you tour the Globe Theatre, Bath, and Hampton Court Palace on your own. It will be the start of embracing your introverted nature and the first step in realizing that as much as you love people, quiet moments alone are essential to your sanity. It is a lesson you will learn over and over again the more complicated your life gets.

Your love for theater will multiply, and most of the money you saved over months of serving tables will be spent on travel and theatre tickets. And when your great-aunt has a layover and treats you out to dinner and a show, you will thoroughly impress her with just how easily you navigate London, the re-emergence of your city girl roots preparing you for eventual moves to three major US cities.

You and your American classmates will teach your English class-mates about the essential nature of s'mores during a bonfire while they teach you about Guy Fawkes Day and the festivities unfolding around you. When you finally sit down to watch V for Vendetta, *it will actually make sense to you. But that won't be the only thing that you finally understand: "Pissing the night away" in the song "Tubthumping," the versatility of the term "cheers," the tension between the English and everyone else of British descent, and the beauty of a well-organized public transportation system. All of those things are just snapshots of the lessons that will change the way you talk about and react to the world around you, reminding you that the more you know, the more you realize you don't know anything.*

You'll eat the British attempt at Thanksgiving dinner (and later long for a chip shop run), celebrate Thanksgiving at a pub, and eventually decide that you can't take anymore lamb and do the super touristy thing by visiting Hard Rock Cafe so you can have an American hamburger.

You'll learn that vodka can be mixed with nearly any juice and be pretty tasty, you'll drink straight whiskey in Ireland, and no matter how hard you try, you will never learn to appreciate the taste of beer, preferring instead the newly launched Smirnoff Ice (which you will spend years looking for in the US before it finally arrives long after you can legally drink).

You'll do all of this and more.

When you come home at Christmas, you will be changed. Some of those changes will be subtle, and some you won't notice for years, but you will be stronger, more independent, more open to listening to the stories and experiences of others, and more confident about where you are headed. When you ring in the new millennium with your smuggled Smirnoff Ice, you will be eager to see what the future holds, convinced that it includes a return trip to Europe sooner than later.

And that boy you almost broke up with right before leaving? You'll marry him. You learn how to communicate in those fifteen weeks apart and both of you will grow through the experience. You'll discover that as much as you are loving your experience, someone is missing: your best friend. And while you haven't boarded a plane to cross the ocean since you returned, together you have taken on the United States, your two children convinced that the only good vacation is a vacation that takes them to new places and experiences. You've replicated that Irish hike in Indiana, Michigan, Kentucky, Tennessee, Colorado, Utah, Texas, New Mexico, Arkansas, and every place you've visited in-between.

So congratulations on an adventure you will never forget. It's the beginning of a great story.

Love,

40-something year old Me

Just Another Day

VALENTINE'S DAY.

When we are children, Valentine's Day is so simple. We check classmates' names off of a list, carefully selecting who gets which card (the boys always got the generic messages), and making the appropriate box for collecting all of the disposable candy and messages that come home after a sugar-infused class party.

Then boys and girls start to be more interesting. Suddenly every card's message has to be carefully analyzed for how it will be understood by the recipient. People start giving "special" gifts to their crushes, days-long "relationships" blooming all around, reminding the giftless that they are somehow deficient in the area of love.

During most of my adolescence, Valentine's Day was the worst day of the year.

My boy-crazy nature plagued me through most of my school career. I easily developed friendships with boys, and while I could hold my own with my male classmates, my insides tied in knots as my heart got crushed by one boy after another who saw me as a good friend and nothing more. Every year I longed for a special message from one of those many boys, and every year my crushes lived up to the name.

And the few exceptions to that rule came from unexpected (and undesired) places.

My sixth-grade year one of the class outsiders gave me a special Valentine and professed that he liked me. A nearly friendless transfer student, I was both flattered and repulsed—that was not how I wanted to finally be recognized by my peers. I wilted as I realized that my crush, the boy who I thought was the cutest in the class, was one of those encouraging the boy's advances.

In high school a boy who was totally off my radar approached me in class with candy and a stuffed animal. While he didn't ask me out, he had definitely made his intentions clear. I spent the next several months navigating the messiness of trying to make it clear in the nicest and politest way possible that I wasn't interested in dating him.

But for the most part, my boy-crazy self spent my adolescent Valentine's Days lonely and disappointed in my inability to attract the attention of a boy I was actually interested in.

That all changed my freshman year of college.

I left for college in Nebraska with a plan. I was going 600 miles from home, I was going to meet a boy at school (just like nearly every member of my family had done), I was going to get a degree, and then I was going to get married immediately after graduation to the boy that I met in some randomly romantic way my freshman year of college.

But the summer before I left for college I met a boy. He took me on a date to watch fireworks along the shores of Lake Michigan and in the weeks that followed we spent every moment we could together. He was fun. I liked him. But he didn't fit in the plan.

So despite the constant emails, occasional phone calls, and a return to a rhythm of going on dates (but not dating!) when we both returned home for Thanksgiving and Christmas, I wasn't going to fall in love with him. And I most certainly would not ever, ever, *ever* consider marrying him.

I returned to school for my second semester with a resolve that I had no interest in dating a boy in a Michigan city 700 miles away from where I was in Nebraska. Then on Valentine's Day my roommate and I were awakened by a phone call announcing a delivery. I carried a dozen roses into our dorm room, looked at the note, and freaked out. They were from him. We weren't dating. I didn't want to be in love with him. I had other plans.

Over the next 10 months we were the epitome of teenage stupidity. Let's just say we were the perfect example of how *not* to cultivate a healthy young adult relationship.

By the next year, we had at least figured out that we were willing to *try* a long-distance relationship, which meant that I was no longer single on the most dreaded day of the year.

The only problem was my boyfriend was several states away and he had to somehow top the dozen roses that he had sent me before we were even dating.

He did.

He drove through the night across the cold and snowy Midwest to surprise me the following morning. Lonely and a little depressed the night before, I had tried to call him just to talk, only to be told by his less-than-observant roommate, "He's on his way to Nebraska to see his girlfriend." Apparently I hadn't had enough phone interaction with this particular roommate for him to know that *I* was the girlfriend he was coming to visit.

We didn't have cell phones. I couldn't verify whether he really was on his way. I had no idea where on I-80 my boyfriend was. I had no way to gauge how far away he was or when he would arrive. I would just have to wait for him to call so my roommate and I could sneak him up to our dorm room during morning non-visiting hours.

While our Valentine's history got an awkward start, for the next three Valentine's Days his gift was his presence, for two years a drive and for the final year a flight into Omaha, so that I didn't have to spend the weekend closest to Valentine's Day alone.

By the time we got married and shared a bank account, the day was just another day. Jeff ordered me flowers once, early in our marriage, and when I saw how much it cost and looked at our nearly bare bank account I quickly assured him that while I greatly appreciated the gesture, I didn't need anything special ever again. And I meant it.

That's not to say that we haven't done things for each other on the holiest of card holidays,[1] but we stopped going out of our way to make the day special.

I don't begrudge those who enjoy celebrating Valentine's Day with all of the bells and whistles. It is wrong to say that I "outgrew" something I know is special to a lot of people, and I believe we should find every way possible to celebrate the love in our lives. But we've decided that we don't need to do something special for each other or prove the lasting intensity of our love story on a specific day that was picked by someone else.

Even more important to me is that our kids see us professing our love for each other every day through our words, our insistence on leaving them with a sitter for dates when they were younger and alone now that they are old enough, and "ew" inducing displays of affection. We've worked hard to show them the importance of pursuing a love that is about more than just a day.

I know it's easy to say that now that I'm a happily married woman. After more Valentine's Days together than apart, it seems trite to tell those lonely in singlehood, "Don't worry about it. It's not that big of a deal." I know that someday soon it won't matter what I say to my daughter as she watches her peers exchange gifts and treasures. A couple years after that we will have to deal with a boy navigating the same waters.

But for us it really is just a day.

I don't want my husband to buy me something expensive because someone many years ago decided that there should be one day a year to shower your significant other with adoration. I don't want to feel obligated to go out on a date with my husband, especially if it means fighting crowds (our least favorite thing). I don't want my son to believe that showing he loves someone is dependent on the kind of gift he gives a girl on one specific day

---

1. In a later chapter I discuss how one year, he did get me flowers after he had to be out of town for work on the same week that I came down with the flu.

of the year. I don't want my daughter's self-worth to be tied up in what she does (or does not) receive on February 14.

So for us, it's just a day. And I'm ok with that. I promise.

Who I Was Created to Be

WHEN I WAS A little girl, my primary dream was to someday be a stay-at-home mom with a large family. Even as my career aspirations changed from teacher to nurse to church youth director and back to teacher, I always knew that I was going to stay at home with my babies, possibly returning to teaching after our many kids were in school full time.

And it's no wonder that I had these dreams. In my family, my grandmothers, my mom, and most of my aunts stayed home with their offspring. I learned that it wasn't just expected; a mom staying home as a primary caregiver was the best and preferable arrangement for *all* families. My life experience taught me to pity my classmates who had moms who worked and had to provide for their families instead of being at home with their children, where they belonged. I considered the few times I had to stay after school with my latchkey peers an injustice. My mother was supposed to be able to take care of me during any time of the day, and that included picking me up from school immediately after we were dismissed.

The gradual change to those dreams started my freshman year of high school, when I turned from being a simple book lover to a literature lover. I no longer just loved reading, I loved reading things worth talking about. By the end of my freshman year I didn't just want to be any teacher, I wanted to be a high school English teacher, a desire that grew every year as my English teachers challenged me and encouraged my intellectual growth. Regardless, the plan was still to get married right after graduation, work for a couple of years, and then start having babies.

God has a funny sense of humor. It's one thing to have an idea of the life you are going to have, often based on the influences of your upbringing, but then life happens. As I've said, Jeff was not some boy I met at college. He didn't fit into the plan at all.

Then I fell in love with learning. I had always loved reading and the new knowledge that came with it, but now I had an unquenchable thirst to know everything I possibly could. I took Russian History and was perfectly satisfied with a B– because I learned so much in the class that my perfectionist self was okay with a less-than-satisfactory grade. I had learned too much to be angry about it. I wanted to know more about everything, each book and course sending me down new paths of discovery. Before I even graduated from college, I knew that once I had a bachelor's degree, I wasn't done going to school.

Then I started teaching and discovered that I was decent at it. I had much to learn, but, like most teachers, I got a lot of on-the-job training. I started thinking that I might stay home with our kids but I would definitely start graduate school so I could keep growing and learning while I was staying at home. After all, it would help me stay sharp so that I would be ready to return to the classroom as soon as my yet-unplanned babies arrived on the scene. I unexpectedly started doubting that I would be completely happy to stay at home with our babies and the number of desired babies started to slowly decrease.

Then I moved to a different school and didn't just discover that I was good at my job, but I *loved* it as well. We couldn't get pregnant right away and I was almost 30 when our first baby was born. We moved again, and I started grad school and then started thinking about all the possibilities once I graduated with my master's degree in English. Then I got pregnant with our son, had a miserable pregnancy, and decided that for the sake of my body and our family's sanity, we needed to be done having kids.

Everything was happening all at once, and we struggled financially to keep all of our bills paid on time. To right the ship, I needed to find a full-time job while I finished the last of my graduate courses. I did, and my love for our small children and for teaching grew alongside each other. I treasured every moment watching my babies grow up, but school was where I felt intellectually challenged and refreshed. I went into high school education because I enjoyed the conversation and interaction with emerging young adults. My instructional time during the day allowed me to appreciate the new milestones with my littles when I was home at night. Summer breaks allowed me to spend more valuable time with my family while also affirming what my husband and I both already knew: I am personally a better, more emotionally and mentally stable mother when I am also working.

Motherhood has changed every woman I know. No one knows how life is going to change after motherhood until she holds *her* baby in her arms and then brings that little one home. I know driven, career-focused women who have dropped everything to stay at home with their little ones because they can't imagine doing anything else. I also know women who have struggled with the decision to go back to work and have eventually made complete peace with being working moms. And I know women who have found space in between, successfully pursuing their professional passions at home while their little ones play around them.

The two most important vocations in my life, being a mother and being a teacher, have made me who I am, and I truly believe that I am the mother and the teacher that I am today because I am doing both at the same time. As a teacher mom, my kids have grown up going in and out of classrooms. I had my daughter near the end of a school year, which actually shortened my necessary maternity leave. While I technically had the whole summer to recuperate and work on planning for the next school year with my infant daughter by my side, that also meant that a month after she was born I was carrying her into end-of-the-year meetings, letting her sleep in her car seat or passing her along to my many colleagues who were eager to hold a sleeping baby.

Are there times that I struggle to maintain the balance? Absolutely. But another episode of Jen Hatmaker's *For the Love* podcast caused me to rethink how I look at my life as a working mother. Jessica Turner discussed her new book *Stretched Too Thin* and she argued that instead of working to maintain a balance (because a perfect balance is unachievable), moms of all kinds need to instead seek work/life satisfaction.[1] I quickly adjusted my thinking at the beginning of the next school year. I made my goal satisfaction as opposed to balance and that has made a difference, at least in my personal outlook. I still struggle, and I still screw up. There are weeks when I'm just happy I have lesson plans done for the day, my family has food to eat because I've at least gone grocery shopping, and I'm not stepping over clutter at home. I understand there are times I have to put more energy in one thing over another, but in the end, I am satisfied in my vocations which keep me a spiritually and mentally healthy mom and teacher.

Do I still occasionally feel guilty about the life choices I've made for myself and my family? Yes. It's hard to let go of the dreams and goals of the past, especially when others aren't completely supportive of the path you have chosen. Sometimes I still feel the need to justify my decision to be a working mom, a decision that at different stages of motherhood was as much about survival as it was about personal fulfillment. My personal growth came when I let go of what I knew to be the expectations of others and embraced what I knew was best for me and my family. In the end, I know what and who I was created to be, and that is what brings me peace.

---

1. "Working Moms Stretched Too Thin: Jessica Turner on Work-Life Satisfaction." *For the Love Podcast*, created by Jen Hatmaker, season 10, episode 4, 14 Aug 2018.

What the Test Says I Am

THE FIRST TIME I ever took a personality test was a left/right brain quiz in my high school psychology class. According to the questionably scientific test, I was bi-lateral—nearly equal parts left and right-brained.

For a girl who was good at math but preferred reading and writing, it actually made perfect sense.

In the years since, I've taken many personality tests. Some were required, like the Myers/Briggs I took in college (at the time I tested as ISFJ), and some I have taken for fun (like the Harry Potter quiz that wisely put me into House Ravenclaw). But each one has given me better insight into who I am as a human being and how to better use my personality traits, viewing them as strengths and not weaknesses.

In Jen Hatmaker's book *Fierce, Free, and Full of Fire*, she writes that personality tests create a self-awareness that "disrupts unhealthy patterns, instructs our decisions, strengthens our relationships, and illuminates our lanes."[1] I have seen that over and over again in my life.

Several years ago, I attended a Love Languages Bible study at my church. At the time I was just looking for a way to get back into scripture and connect with people outside of work and home. I had some reservations about using the Love Languages as a guide for how I relate to my faith, but I was willing to take the quiz and learn alongside others in the study.

---

1. Jen Hatmaker, *Fierce, Free, Fire*, p. 13-14

It didn't just change the way I looked at my faith study, it changed the way that I looked at my own family.

I learned that my primary Love Language is acts of service, which kind of felt obvious once I learned what that entailed, but it also explained why I was so irritated when my loving husband would try to shower me with kisses when all I really wanted was for him to volunteer to do the dishes without me asking. And while experts will repeatedly tell hobby analysts to avoid typing their family members, it became more obvious to both of us that our son's love languages are touch and gifts and our daughter's is acts of service. Taking those traits into consideration gave me a new way to understand and relate to my children, helping to strengthen our interactions, and even our discipline, with each child.

I've also learned that life can impact our personality typing. When I was a college student, I initially tested as an ISFJ, although my introversion barely surpassed my extroversion. In more recent years, I've switched sensing for feeling while becoming more introverted. While my INFJ typing is pretty accurate to how I see and react to the world now, life experience has played a huge role in even the slightest changes.

For years I felt like being an introvert instead of a clear extrovert handicapped me in every area of my life, but as I've gotten older I've also learned to embrace that part of my personality and use it to my advantage. I dove into reading Susan Cain's book *Quiet* to help me better understand myself, but it really helped me better understand my whole world. Reading Cain's book helped me to see the potential strengths behind introversion. I learned that it is not a weakness to be overcome but a strength to be utilized for better interaction with the world around me. More importantly, everything I have learned has helped me better relate to my own very introverted daughter.

One of my more recent personality growth projects has been diving into the Enneagram. Experience has taught me how useful digging into my personality traits can be in helping me better understand the hows and whys of the way I respond to the world around me. The more I learn about the Enneagram, the more I see how understanding a clear description of my personality actually helps me to better see myself.

While I tried taking several free tests on the topic over the last year, every time I took a quiz the results didn't match the way I saw myself. I know we often avoid being honest with ourselves, but I read each typing with as critical an eye as possible, and it just didn't seem right. I finally caved to a friend's pressure and decided to read up on the topic and go from there.

Reading *The Road Back to You* by Ian Morgan Cron and Suzanne Stabile had the same impact as reading *Quiet*. I wasn't looking for some kind of diagnosis to figure out what was wrong with me. I was trying to discover how to better understand how I move in the world. Cron and Stabile's book helped me to finally dig into the nine different Enneagram types and truly figure out where I fit.

So where do I fit? I'm a clear One, the Perfectionist. The more I read about the One, the more I see it, both as a conviction in the parts about myself that I abhor and in recognizable strengths.

In the Enneagram, there is also a wing, which means you naturally adopt the traits of one of the numbers next to yours in the circle and you grow to adopt the other number later in life. After reading through both, it became painfully clear that I am a Nine wing, the Peacemaker.

Reading about the Peacemaker I felt like I was repeatedly getting hit over the head. Reading about the Perfectionist I felt like I had been plowed over by a truck. The painful truth about being a peacemaking perfectionist is that I am introverted and often detached, thinking through my responses for too long and spending too much time mulling over my decisions. I want my decisions to be perfectly planned out, but I also don't want people to be mad at me for whatever decision I make. It explains my tendency to procrastinate and allow things (like my dirty kitchen table) to go neglected when I'm feeling stressed.

This awareness of my personality type became important in ways I couldn't possibly understand when I lost a job that I loved at the beginning of 2021. Everything related to the job loss ate away at my perfectionist self, while my One need for justice and righting what was wrong overpowered my Nine wing's desire for peace. It also explained my response to our current political landscape, as I have an innate desire for everyone to just do the right thing and have to temper my righteous anger with a desire for all of society to just get along.

And yes, being a One with a Nine wing can be more than a little exhausting.

Some people believe that the danger of personality typing is that we are too quick to fall back on it and blame it for every issue we have, but it doesn't have to be that way. Really digging into well-researched personality typing (*not* our horoscope or astrological sign) can help us to better function, if we are willing to be honest with ourselves and do the work.

I have found that personality typing has been a helpful tool that gives me information I can use to more effectively deal with the world around me. I just try to avoid jumping onto *every* tool that comes my way.

Place

Closure Matters

I'VE SAID A LOT of goodbyes.

Whether or not those goodbyes were by choice, it was always important to ensure some kind of closure. I have years' worth of handwritten messages, gifts, and photographs from a lifetime of goodbyes from every stage of growth and change.

Some approach closure with an act of finality, closing all doors and moving on without looking back. I've always preferred to see closure as the act of ending one era before beginning a new one. It doesn't mean I forget the era or the people involved. It definitely doesn't mean that I never speak to those people again and completely cut them out of my life. It just means that I have successfully executed a clean break that allows me to move forward, as opposed to remaining immovably rooted in the past.

Closure hasn't always been easy for me. When we moved to Fort Wayne a year after our daughter was born, I didn't make a clean break from Indianapolis.

At the time, I was teaching a couple of classes I felt unprepared to teach, making me uncomfortable in my classroom two periods a day. I was a new mom trying to figure out the balance between mommyhood and work. I had dreams of what my last show as a theater director was going to be and was forced to consider other options. Relationships with students whom I had been close to became strained during that decision-making process and the following production. And on top of all of that, I was dealing with the emotional stress of moving compounded by the realities of life, such as a house that wouldn't sell in a depressed market and lack of professional direction for me.

We also never scheduled an official departure. I tried to clean out my classroom, but it got cleaned out for me in preparation for new carpeting, so I just moved the boxes that had been placed in the hallway. Over the next five years of sorting and cleaning while we lived in Fort Wayne, we found random items that should have never left with us, including keys, books, and classroom items that didn't belong to me. When we prepared for our move, we didn't pack up a moving truck and move everything in one fell swoop. Instead, we made multiple trips, driving over 200 miles round trip to pick up whatever we could fit in our vehicles from our yet-unsold house and taking those items to our new house, which was in various stages of repair. There was never a formal "goodbye" to our friends because we kept coming back for a host of reasons. It didn't really feel like we had left. It was almost as if we were taking several mini-vacations away.

When we moved to Texas from Fort Wayne, it felt like we experienced healthy closure. I had "last" lunches with colleagues and friends as the school year came to a close. My classroom was empty, and I did all the sorting, cleaning, tossing, and packing myself. My students boosted my ego with many notes (and a couple of gifts) letting me know how much I would be missed. We actually sold our house. When the moving truck pulled up and emptied our house, nothing was left behind. We took our memories and our closest friendships with us, sharing with those who mattered most to us the new adventures we were having in a new state.

I feel a strange sense of disconnect when I think of the closure on our latest transition from Houston back to Indianapolis. The lack of closure from a job I loved and students I cared for left me feeling ungrounded. I didn't know what I was supposed to do or feel or even who I could talk to about that feeling of disconnect. When we finally made the decision to change our lives—again—and move back to Indianapolis, closure arrived as a definitive decision. Once again, we sold our house, I found a new job, we bought a new house, and we picked up the lives we had left behind eleven years before. Yes, life was different than it was when we were young. Yes, we opened a new chapter. But it felt right in ways I could not have predicted before 2020 changed all of our lives.

Closure matters. It keeps us emotionally and mentally healthy and allows us to move on to the next stage of our lives. It gives us the freedom to let go, leap, and let God lead our next steps.

But to be honest, that is easier said than done.

When History Repeats Itself

OUR CHILDHOOD EXPERIENCES SHAPE the kinds of lives we want our children to live. Many of us want our kids to have what we didn't have, and we *don't* want our kids to have the same negative experiences we had. We work so hard to replicate our best memories and avoid repeating what we perceive to be our parents' biggest mistakes. Of course, we usually don't realize how difficult these desires are in practice until we are living in the moments that will shape our children's lives.

My dad was a Lutheran church worker, and he moved more often than he stayed. By the time I turned eighteen, I had lived in four states, four time zones, and five different cities or towns. I don't remember the move from California to Michigan when I was one, but then we moved when I was nine, eleven, and sixteen. When I was nine it wasn't *so* bad. It was exciting, and while I missed my old friends, I quickly made new ones. The girls in my fourth-grade class were still nice enough to let me join their circle.

If only I could say that about the next two moves that turned my adolescent world upside down.

Both times I needed my old friends to remember me as I remembered them. I wanted them to miss me as much as I missed them; they were more concerned about the here and now of their lives. I got letters and occasional phone calls (in the age of paying for long-distance phone calls by the minute), but it wasn't the same as having them there with me whenever I needed or wanted them.

When I headed off to college to pursue a degree in secondary education, I swore to myself that I would never do that to my own children. After all, I was going to be a high school teacher. They don't move around, right? I wanted to get married and have a stable career. I wanted to stay in one place and be settled. I wanted my own children to be able to grow up and graduate with their best friends. I wanted my kids to see the country, but only on family vacations, not because they were being moved from one coast to the other.

But life hasn't been that way. Jeff and I made our first big move when it was clear we weren't happy with where we were geographically and professionally. We moved two hours away to a different city and different jobs. Then, after five years in the same location, that job he had found moved us another two hours away. For five more years we tried to make the next move work, and professionally it was really good for both of us. Our two children had friends and schools that they loved. But while I made some good friendships, I never planted roots.

So for a couple of years we talked about the possibility of moving. We had talked about the different scenarios that would lead to us moving and had discussed where we would want to go if we did move. But making that decision was a different story. My husband had a good job with plenty of job security where he was loved and admired—so much so that even with two more moves since living in Fort Wayne, he is still working for the same company. I loved the school where I taught for four years. We were where we were supposed to be, and I had to trust that we were doing what we were supposed to be doing. And while I never felt like I was home, it also never felt like God was saying, "This is it."

And then we took the huge leap of faith to move our midwestern selves to Houston. Suddenly I was committing the parenting crime I swore I would never commit. I was planning to move my kids away from friends, farther away from grandparents and some cousins, and away from the only life that they had ever really known. It was now or never. Our kids were four and six, just old enough to have attachments but young enough to easily make friends in nearly any situation. But that didn't make it an easy summer. Our daughter said several "good-byes" to friends with play dates, time at Vacation Bible School, and repeated trips up to Michigan. Our son felt left out during those good-bye sessions which led to tears and finally an evening with his best friend, which ended in late-night tears. After they sat through the hour-long house closing session, our son dissolved into tears telling us that he didn't want us to sell our house and wanted us to buy it back. Both kids had moments of sadness, and our son's normally mischievous behavior turned frustratingly belligerent.

It has not been easy to watch my own children experience many of the feelings of loss that I have experienced at various points in my life. Some days, like when my son had to say goodbye to his best friend, were downright painful. No one wants their kids to feel pain of any kind, but I also know it is an inevitable reality of life.

During all of this I felt guilty. Guilty for looking forward to the future, guilty for wanting to move despite the disruption to our family's life. I wanted this to be the end of the road for my family. My husband and I agreed that we wanted to settle and find a home and make it home. I prayed it was the last time.

And then it wasn't.

Six years later we were facing many of the same struggles and questions, only this time with children entering the troubled waters of adolescence. We didn't take our decision to move back to Indianapolis lightly. We didn't want to leave behind the best parts of living in Houston, and we didn't want to take our kids away from the lives they had built with friends who mattered very deeply to them. But our dreams were changed for us, and that meant moving despite the immediate cost to our family.

Someday my children will forgive me, I hope. I've forgiven my parents (mostly) for all of the changes through my childhood. For better or worse, it made me who I am today. It made me a mother who wants stability for her children. But I also understand, as an adult, that stability has to be there for all members of the family, and change, big and small, is inevitable. What matters is how the family responds to the change.

It's been over a year since our family's most recent big change, and we continue to grow and heal and see all that is good and hard through a move to a place our kids didn't want to know.

So while I wish the echoes of my past had stayed out of my life as a mother, I am thankful that we are still sticking with each other through it all. It makes even the most difficult changes at least a little more tolerable.

Emotions of Change

OUR FAMILY HAS HAD a love affair with the Harry Potter series since Jeff and I got married. In *The Order of the Phoenix*, in between Ron and Hermione's increasing tension, the formation of Dumbledore's Army, Occlumency lessons, the horrors of Dolores Umbridge, Harry seeing inside Voldemort's head, the building of a Death Eater Army, and preparation for the O.W.L.s, J.K. Rowling wrote a poignant scene involving the three best friends in which they discuss Harry's first kiss with Cho Chang. Cho started crying after they kissed, and when Harry tells his friends what happened, Ron suggests Harry must just be a bad kisser. Hermione offers a different suggestion, listing the many complicated feelings that Cho had to be feeling, including still grieving over Cedric's death. When she finishes, Ron responds, "One person can't feel all that at once, they'd explode."[1] It is just one more example of the series' ability to capture the complexity of human emotions.

Life changes always bring out our strongest emotions, and sometimes the worst of those emotions come spilling out of us at the most inopportune times. Unfortunately, we don't really give each other permission to honestly *feel* our emotions, and this is something I keep learning over and over again as a mom who has seen how geographic changes have impacted our family over and over again.

---

1. J.K. Rowling, *Harry Potter and the Order of the Phoenix*, p. 459

Inside Out came out right before our family moved to Texas and it might have hit a little too close to home. In the movie, eleven-year-old Riley moves with her family from Minnesota to San Francisco. We watch her emotions (through the distinctive characters Joy, Sadness, Anger, Disgust, and Fear) learn to work together as Riley tries to cope with the emotions related to a huge life change. Her mother asks her to be brave for her father, who has his own struggles with the move that is affecting his family. We watch Riley bottle her emotions and, in the process, implode, leading to her eventual pre-adolescent decision to run away because Minnesota was the last place where she was happy.

Joy discovers that she can't work on her own. We can't be happy all of the time. Sometimes we need the other emotions to balance us out and bring us back to Joy. As our family watched the movie in the movie theater, I felt like I was watching my childhood play out before my eyes. Our then-six-year-old daughter felt like she was living the movie in real time.

Our six-year-old daughter cried as she watched an older girl deal with the same complex emotions that she had been experiencing. She was excited about the changes ahead, but she knew there was a lot she was going to miss. Watching the movie opened up a lot of discussion for our family; we told our daughter that she was not only allowed to be sad, but she needed to let us know when she was sad. It gave us the opportunity to validate her feelings and let her know that the most important thing for her to do was to be honest with us and to not try to hide her emotions.

It was an important lesson we would have to repeat six years later when we moved back to Indiana.

I learned to bottle my emotions when my family moved to Wyoming. At the tender age of 11, I kept every struggle to myself: missing my friends, being bullied, feeling completely alone. I spent too much time trying to keep my parents happy so they wouldn't worry about me and could work on their own healing in a new place. Eventually I learned to love Wyoming and all it had to offer, but I also became an expert at keeping my true feelings to myself, something that still plagues me in middle age.

But the changes didn't end there.

We moved from Wyoming to Michigan the summer before my junior year from high school. It also was the summer that I had my very first boyfriend, a boy I met at a summer youth event. He lived in Illinois, and I believed that he would be just close enough that we could make long distance work. I believed I was in love with this boy whom I had known for only a week. When I told my mom I was in love with him she brushed it off. I was only 16; I didn't know what love was. Looking back, I can see the absurdity of the situation. I didn't love him, and the relationship was doomed to fail from the start. But I was sad, I was lonely, I missed my friends, and I just needed something to believe in.

Eight months later, when a close friend in Wyoming died by suicide, I chose to bottle most of my emotions. I cried, but I didn't know what else to say or how to say it, and 25 years later I'm still seeking the closure that I desperately needed at 16. I needed to be encouraged to talk and share with people who got it. Instead, I kept most of my thoughts and fears and emotions to myself, pretending that everything was okay even when it wasn't.

I've always wanted better for my own kids.

Nothing prepared me for how difficult our first big move as a family would be. Our son, at four, was devastated in the final weeks leading up to the move. His toys were packed, he had to say goodbye to his friends, and he had to leave behind the only home he had ever known. Our arrival in Texas didn't make it much easier. We lived in our camper while we waited for our home loan to be finalized, and he missed his space and some of his favorite toys. When we were getting ready to meet his preschool teacher, he adamantly announced that he didn't want to go to school and he didn't need new friends. He just wanted to go back to "Indianana." For well over a month, he constantly talked about wanting to go back to the only state that had ever been home.

On the other hand, our daughter was surprisingly upbeat. She kept asking about the start of school, eager for a routine and kids her own age. But her upbeat facade crumbled at Meet the Teacher. She didn't want to talk to anyone, she closed in on herself, and then she got insistent on having something to draw on and something to draw with. I ignored the signals. I told her that if she didn't stop acting that way we weren't going to go to the ice cream social being held for the new families.

Then the floodgates opened. My little girl suddenly sobbed in my arms. Her first-grade teacher graciously gave her the desired art supplies, and our little girl sat down at her desk and drew a picture and wrote a note for her best friend from kindergarten. Suddenly it all made sense. Our little art and composition-loving introvert needed to get her feelings out the only way she knew how: on paper. Instead of being angry, I had to pull my tearful self together to thank her teacher for giving her the necessary supplies.

I had to remind myself of these painful moments as we worked to adjust to a new home six years later. I didn't want my kids to learn to keep everything inside or to avoid telling us their struggles because they were trying to stay out of my way. I didn't want them to feel responsible for my own healing as I also made difficult adjustments through a move that I wanted and they did not.

So we tolerated a lot of sulking and tears. We allowed our son to play too many video games so that he could talk to friends from Texas and our daughter to spend too much time on her new phone messaging and talking to her friends 1000 miles away. We told them to tell us when they were struggling, even if we didn't like what we were hearing. And I'll be honest—there were times we didn't like what we were hearing.

But a year later, after the kids and I returned from a trip back to visit friends, we hit a rhythm. Our son was happy to return to friends, and our daughter eagerly started attending a new school where she started to thrive in ways we hadn't seen in well over a year. And we kept talking. We kept doors of communication open. We know that we weren't perfect parents through another difficult transition, but we did our best. I just hope that they are able to see that someday.

Unexpected Changes, Unexpected Timeline

"Do you regret moving to Texas?"

Jeff's question hit like a ton of bricks. Did I regret the move that had changed our lives in so many positive ways but had, in the end, caused us a considerable amount of emotional and spiritual pain?

No.

I didn't regret it.

But I was ready to return "home."

I had never wanted to leave Indianapolis, the closest to home we had ever been in our nearly twenty years of marriage. While we were only there for five years, we spent those five years building strong friendships, truly starting our careers, and starting our family when we brought home our daughter.

Hindsight is 20/20. While our move to Fort Wayne turned me into a thirty-year-old petulant child who wasn't getting her way, that also was a good and necessary move. It furthered both of our careers in ways neither of us could have ever imagined. Although our fixer-upper house was a challenge to our marriage and bank account, we learned many invaluable lessons over the five years of renovation. And we were stronger than ever as a family unit.

But if I couldn't move back to Indianapolis and I just couldn't stay in Fort Wayne, we needed a big change as a family, and it had to come before our kids were too old for us to do permanent damage.

So we moved to Texas.

Our lives are richer because of the six years we lived in Texas. Jeff and I saw our careers improve and expand in ways we had never imagined before. We saw parts of the country that we never would have considered had we not left the Midwest and moved down to the South.

But the prospect of staying was too painful. The hurt too real. The need for "our people" too strong.

Staying was no longer an option.

In a two week span we went from "let's start looking at moving back to Indianapolis on a twelve-month timeline to make sure all of our ducks are in a row," to me applying for jobs in Indianapolis because I still didn't have a job in Houston, to me interviewing for two positions, to me accepting one that would start just over a month later.

Twelve months became six weeks. The future became right now. And there were moments when it felt like our world was going to spin right off of its axis.

Moving is never convenient. Change is never easy.

We had just bought solar panels. We loved our solar panels. We had finally moved into the twenty-first century of green tech just as the Texas power grid was threatening to fail, again. We loved our warm winters. And the Texas state parks. And there were so many things that we still hadn't seen or visited.

But the material can't replace the need to be where we have a strong support system and a closer proximity to family. Our appreciation for many of the things we had in Texas never replaced the longing to walk along the Lake Michigan shoreline and watch the sun set across the vast body of water. It didn't take away the pangs I felt every time I saw the Indianapolis skyline on television when we watched the Colts play. It didn't stop us from wishing we could be camping in Brown County State Park every Halloween or visiting our other favorite Indiana and Michigan state parks.

So we did what I swore I would never do. As parents we all know that we are going to cause our kids inadvert pain. We know we are going to have to make decisions that will break their hearts and sometimes their spirits. We know that we won't be perfect at every turn.

But that knowledge doesn't make the reality any easier.

I moved when I was going into the fourth grade, same as my son was as we planned our move back to Indianapolis. While that move worked out great for me, I remember the early days of mourning the loss of my best friend next door whom I had known since I was a baby. I missed my neighbor across the street. I missed my other best friends whom I would have seen again at school with the return of fall.

I moved when I was in sixth grade. My daughter was going into seventh. My middle school years were miserable, and I feared the same for my daughter, but she had an amazing sixth grade year with friends who knew and loved her and truly cared for her heart. I wanted that to be her middle school experience for three years. I didn't want to disrupt her world. And that's exactly what I did as my husband and I sat down and tearfully told them that Mom had finally found a job, but it was nowhere near where our little girl wanted to be.

Knowing that the benefits of a change far outweigh all the reasons not to doesn't make the pain and confusion and loss of control any less significant. We can know that something is good for us while still grieving the losses that come with it.

Our whole family had to work to accept the highly unexpected in our lives during the summer of 2021, and it wasn't easy.

Suddenly we found ourselves with only days to get our house ready to put on the market before we left for vacation. We had less than a week to finish the packing and move once we returned from vacation. While our previous moves had involved months of planning and then a rush at the very end to get everything taken care of, our whole last move happened in a rush. A rush that felt right, but a rush nonetheless.

Those months following the most rushed decision in our lives were heartbreaking and often soul-crushing, but I never stopped believing that we had made the right decision. I never stopped praying for the light I knew was at the end of the tunnel.

But it was dark there for a moment, and would continue to be until we all finally felt like we were, once again, home.

Lessons From Texas

Our move to Texas in 2015 was supposed to be a move from the Midwest to our new "forever" home. After nearly a lifetime of living in the cold winters and unpredictable summers, we were ready to see what warm winters and predictably hot summers would hold. We wanted to see new parts of the country. And we saw opportunities available for us in the South that we didn't have at that moment in the North.

So we headed to the Lone Star State.

Before our move back to the Midwest, when Jeff asked me if I regretted our move to Texas, I had to think for a moment before I gave him an honest "no." We had a good five years there, and the sixth year was rough for a pile of different reasons. But those good five years, and the good moments in that sixth year, just highlighted the many things—positive and negative—we learned about our temporarily-adopted state.

We learned that everything really is bigger in Texas. The cities are bigger, more people own bigger trucks, the gas stations are bigger (and our family rarely refused a chance to go to Buc-ee's), the roads are bigger, the food portions are bigger...I could really go on and on. And I'm honestly not sad that my children will not be tempted to participate in the Homecoming tradition of "Mums and Garters." (And if you don't know what that is, Google it.)

But all that bigger is honestly reflective of the second largest state in the nation. Texas is huge. We learned this fact traveling to Big Bend National Park twice, as we had to take two days just to safely get to the park. We've learned this reality on two vacations to the American West, as it took us more than two days to just leave the state. We learned this truth as we traveled along the I-10 corridor to vacations out east, the interstate highway totaling 878 miles from one end of Texas to the other. We became accustomed to spending three or more hours on the road to visit new cities and state parks, and that is without us venturing past central Texas.

Texas is just big, period.

We learned that Texas is not all one thing, and Texans are not all one people.

We heard a lot of jokes from friends and family in the Midwest as we planned for our move to Texas. Jeff was going to come back with boots and a belt buckle, we were all going to pick up ridiculous accents, and moving to Texas meant liberation from the rest of the country.

We learned the significance of belt buckles (and no one in our family was interested); good cowboy boots are both expensive and last forever (and yes, both Jeff and I still each have a pair because I'm a sucker for boots of any kind); had been saying "y'all" long before we moved; and just because Texas likes to see itself as independent, it doesn't mean that its way of doing things is always best (a reality that really hit home during the breakdown of ERCOT during the February 2021 winter storm that left most of the state frozen and without power for several days).

To the outside world, Texas seems to be a backward "red" state with people who are consistently acting against their own interests. We've learned that the state, and her people, are so much more complicated than that. Texas is varying shades of purple, with red and blue dots scattered throughout. The energy sector is oil and gas and nuclear and wind and solar, all trying to figure out where they fit in the grand scheme of things. Immigrants from all over the world are spread around the state, making the cities diverse and challenging the traditional stereotypes. We went to the Houston Rodeo only once, and I saw a woman wearing a cowboy hat over a hijab and I couldn't have seen anything more representative of Houston in that given moment.

And it's not just the people. We saw the desert canyon of Palo Duro, the river valley along Big Bend, and alligators in the local swamplands. The Texas ecosystem is just as diverse as her people, and it makes the state all the more beautiful. That incredible biodiversity also drives the diversity in experience, beliefs, and the views of her millions of people.

We learned the hard way that fire ants are the spawn of Satan.

I do not exaggerate. I heard stories about fire ants, I heard their bites were painful, I knew that the numbers increase the further south one went, I knew that my feet would no longer be perfectly safe in the green grass.

But I didn't know. Not really. I didn't know the pain of that sting, the bubbling blister as my skin reacted to the poison, the painful itch that could last for weeks afterward.

Then our daughter found an ant pile in a Target parking lot during our *first* week living in Houston. Her blood-curdling scream indicated just how painful it could be. Then I got my first bite, then my second, and then my third experience put my overheated body in an urgent care clinic with hives that covered my body from head to toe.

I have no positive spin to put on fire ants. They are terrible. They serve no purpose. I was thrilled to get back to my Kentucky bluegrass and ant hills full of insects not intent on killing me, thank you very much.

We learned that you can get acclimated to the heat.

I know it sounds crazy, but just as people up north claim that you can get acclimated to the cold (something I still struggle to accept even after living up north for most of my life), you can get acclimated to the heat. We moved to Texas in July, just as summer really started to heat up. It was hot, and we were living in a travel trailer that had an air conditioning unit suited for Indiana summers, not Texas.

But we learned to appreciate summer nights that get into the low 80s, putting on long sleeves if the night temps dropped below 70. Hot is hot, and I couldn't be found spending much time outside after 11:00 AM, but we learned how to survive, as long as the power stayed on.

We learned that Texas history is incredibly fascinating and frustratingly fraught.

Even before we moved to Texas, we knew that learning Texas history would be far more fascinating than the Indiana history our kids would have been learning or the Michigan or Illinois history we learned as kids. That's not to say that the history of those Midwest states is boring, but it's not nearly as colorful as Texas history from the beginning to today.

We went to Goliad, toured the Alamo, walked aboard the Battleship Texas, visited the state capital, and explored Galveston Island. My kids learned Texas history in school and in our travels and internalized the complicated nature of a state that prides itself on fierce independence while plagued by a history of oppression of racial minorities. The history of Texas is as complex as her people. Texans pride themselves in knowing about Juneteenth before much of the country, while also electing legislatures intent on preventing students from learning the good, the bad, and the ugly of state history.

For an outsider, it is maddening.

While it is a gross oversimplification of a large and incredibly diverse state, it is a state at a crossroads, a crossroads that this Midwesterner decided she would be better off observing from the sidelines.

Our family also found itself at a crossroads, a divergence that took us back to our own roots in the upper Midwest.

I miss the incredible amount of diversity throughout Texas. I miss the exciting places we never visited and the ones we wanted to return to. I miss our pool. I miss wearing a tank top and capris on Christmas morning. I miss camping in 60-degree weather on Thanksgiving. I miss our solar panels and the good we could have done in being alternative energy ambassadors. I miss the friendships that remained once the dust settled.

I do not miss (which I will never take for granted again) and torrential rains that last for days. I do not miss saying a state pledge in the mornings (yes, Texas has its own pledge of allegiance, and, yes, I find it just as weird as it sounds to anyone else who is not from the state). I do not miss the Texas state flag flying at the same height as the American flag or seeing the phrase "Come and get it" on nearly everything (although I finally understand both the historical and modern implication). I do not miss the worst of the heat and the oppressive humidity.

But our lives are richer because of six years in the Lone Star State. My role as an American citizen is more informed and motivated after what I saw and experienced there. And we are stronger as a family for the time we spent exploring and learning together, just the four of us.

For that, I will forever be grateful.

Moving Sucks

WE KNEW BETTER THAN to say never again.

Because our "forever house" kept changing.

Because I grew up with changing definitions of home.

Because there are no guarantees in life.

When we bought our first house in Hobart, Indiana, we knew it wouldn't be our forever home. We were in our early twenties, and children were down the road. We bought a house we believed we could grow into, but we didn't really believe we would want to stay there forever.

Then when we moved to Indianapolis, Indiana, we bought a true "starter home," a house that I worked hard to make ours and a house Jeff never loved. The plan had always been to buy a bigger house when we had more than one kid and make that our forever home.

That is probably why, when we found ourselves transferred to Fort Wayne, we searched for the house that would become our forever home. I didn't want another transition, neither of us wanted to once again do the work that moving required, and we found a house that was a mess but plenty big enough for a growing family with a lot of potential to make it our own.

So when we made the decision to turn our lives upside down and move halfway across the country to Texas, we were clear that we were *never moving again.* We spent six weeks living in our camper as a family of five (four humans and a dog), and even though we had movers to move us out of our Fort Wayne house and carry our stuff 1,000 miles, we weren't that lucky when we moved into our new house on Labor Day weekend. With help from two friends, we took multiple trips between the tightly packed storage unit and our new house, only to have the skies open up on us on our last load, causing our cheap bookshelves to collapse after being doused by rain.

We weren't going to do it again.

We should have learned from *An American Tail* to "Never say never again." We really should have. Because when our lives got turned upside down and I suddenly had to re-evaluate everything I thought I knew about what our lives would be, I fought that nagging desire to move back "home." I fought it with everything I had. I didn't want to leave our house. I didn't want to turn our kids' lives upside down. I didn't want to deal with all of the hassle of buying and selling and packing. I didn't want to run away from the very things that were causing me daily heartache.

But we made the decision anyway. It seemed impulsive. It seemed like we hadn't thought things through. It seemed like we didn't really know what we were doing. But we did. We were just finally giving in to the very thing that had been staring us straight in the face for months.

But even knowing that you are doing the right thing doesn't change the fact that moving sucks.

Leaving behind beloved landmarks sucks. Packing up a house that you invested both money and personal labor into making it a home sucks. Saying goodbye to friends and neighbors who have become "your people" sucks. Watching your kids grieve for lost friends and things sucks. Finding new doctors and dentists and fulfilling all other medical needs sucks. Searching for new places to shop and eat and make a part of your regular life sucks.

We moved ourselves, and if it hadn't been for my mom flying down from Michigan to help us pack, we don't know that we ever would have gotten out of Houston. We moved ourselves into our new residence after waiting an extra two weeks for our stuff to arrive at our house which we put an offer on before we ever had a chance to see it in person. I started my new job twelve hours after arriving at my sister's house, where we stayed for an extra night while we tried to get ourselves situated at a

RV campground that made us even more eager to sign for our new house. Jeff argued with mortgage lenders to ensure that our closing happened on time so we could get situated into a place where we could each have our own space, even though we wouldn't have any of our stuff for at least another week. Our dishwasher broke as soon as we moved in and so the mess that our house was going to become once we had our stuff became exacerbated by the fact that our kitchen was overflowing with dirty dishes if we decided to cook at home.

We spent the first month or so of living in Indianapolis processing through all of the things related to how much moving sucks.

But then most of the boxes were unpacked. I painted bedrooms and bathrooms and the kitchen in colors that matched the desires of each member of the family. Family photos and wall hangings found appropriate locations all over the house. Moving closer meant getting help from a sister and brother-in-law and both sets of parents, all of whom worked to make our house feel so much more like our home so we could get situated earlier.

Yes, moving sucks, but eventually you get to the other side. There were days when it felt like that would never happen, when it felt like our house would never be put together and the kids would never adjust to new friends and a new school and that even though I had found a new job, it was never going to feel like the right job.

But two months after moving we spent a weekend at our daughter's soccer tournament with my sister and her family, and my daughter glowed when she saw her little cousins running towards her as she came off of the field. A year later, our son and nephew have played on the same flag football, soccer, and basketball teams and we've cheered with family on the sidelines. Our parents come down for a quick two-day visit and it isn't a big deal because they are less than a four-hour drive away. Old friends come over and stay late while our kids finally get to know each other in the way we had planned our kids would be able to do when we were just entering our 30s and bringing those same babies into the world.

I hate moving. I hate change. But over my lifetime it has brought me experiences and friendships and an understanding of the world around me that staying in one place would have never given me.

And remembering all of that makes moving suck just a little bit less, maybe.

Missing Photographs

By NOW IT'S PROBABLY clear that I grew up in a somewhat nomadic household.

From the time I was born until the time I graduated from high school, I lived in four different states, we moved five times, and I attended six different schools. I didn't attend the same high school as my childhood friends. I didn't attend the same high school for all four years. I couldn't even apply for National Honor Society until I was a senior because of a move across the country the summer before my junior year.

I know people who lived far more nomadic lifestyles, but mine certainly hadn't been a childhood or adolescence marked by the stability of consistent friendships that spanned my entire academic career.

I wanted it to be different for my own kids. I had dreams for them. I had plans for twelve years of attending the same schools with the same friends from the time they started until the time that they graduated from high school.

When I was a yearbook adviser, I was in charge of collecting senior messages with collages of my very grown-up students during every stage of their lives. As I looked through ads and messages and carefully placed them in spreads, I considered all of the photos from the years that I would want to include in my own message to my graduating children.

Now my husband and I are finally at that age where we are seeing friend after friend posting pictures of their not-so-little ones graduating from high school. While our late venture into parenthood means that we have a few more years to go before we start emptying the nest, we are getting a taste of what it means to prepare for that transition, and, again, I'm looking at photo collages of our friends' children from every stage of their lives. Some of the most adorable collages are the ones that show them with the same friends over the years, through preschool baby cheeks, elementary growth, middle school awkwardness, and finally high school maturity.

After an adolescence and young adulthood of mourning the absence of my own pictures with the same childhood friends through the years, I desperately wanted that for my own children.

That was my dream when we brought our little girl home to the south side of Indianapolis. Then a year later we moved to Fort Wayne. Five years later we moved to Houston and at the young ages of four and six, it appeared that I could somehow keep the dream alive. But six years later we moved back to Indianapolis and the dream I had for both of my children from the time they were born lay shattered at my feet. I would never be able to create cradle-to-graduation-cap collages. I would never know what it was like to watch the same group of children grow alongside my children into young adulthood and see their friendships through all of the changes and challenges of growing up. And they would never know the gift of having friends alongside them who had known them through every stage of childhood.

I don't fault my friends for sharing adorable photos of their now-graduated seniors when they were friends back in kinder-garten. Truth be told, if it were me I would be that annoying mom putting my kids and their best friends through the torture of replicating poses through the years.

It's just the difficult reality for those of us who have exchanged consistent stability in a single geographic location for new and exciting challenges and adventures. One is not better than the other, each decision bringing with it advantages and disadvantages. For me, the biggest challenge has been the loss of personal connection and history. I wish I could have spared my own children the same experiences, but life happens, and we learn how to adjust our expectations to match the lives that we are given.

I'm happy for the friends who have those progressive photographs. I'm glad their children faced a different set of challenges from knowing and being with the same people for their entire childhoods. But for those of us who will never have those photos, who feel a sharp pang every single time we see our friends post those cradle-to-graduation-cap photographs, it can be too difficult a reminder of the things we lost in exchange for experiences.

To those who have cradle-to-graduation consistency, please don't stop sharing, don't stop posting, and do not feel like there is any shame in celebrating the stability that you have been able to give your children from the time you brought them home. Just know that some of us are living vicariously through your photographs, and hoping our own children will someday forgive us for taking away their own chance to graduate with their preschool classmates.

Full Circle to the Circle City

WHEN MY HUSBAND AND I moved to Indianapolis in the summer of 2005, we were in our mid-twenties with our whole lives in front of us. We were Michiganders looking for a new home after three years in Chicagoland, and Indianapolis was the perfect place for us to relocate. It was still a large enough city to give us everything we wanted, but it wasn't nearly as overwhelming as living just forty-five minutes from downtown Chicago.

For five years, we lived in and loved the city of Indianapolis. We attended a few baseball games at Victory Field and hockey games at the Coliseum (where we made jokes that we felt like we were on the movie set for *Chasing Amy*). We jumped on the Colts bandwagon and cheered on their victory over the Chiefs in the AFC Wildcard Game at the RCA Dome. We watched my high school students make a run for the basketball state championship at, what was then, Conseco Fieldhouse. We visited the animals at the zoo in both summer and winter months and listened to Weird Al from the lawn seats in White River State Park. We climbed up the stairs to the third story to watch movies at the now-closed Hollywood Bar and Grill and strolled around Monument Circle. I visited the Children's Museum with a friend and our new babies. While we didn't take advantage of all Indianapolis had to offer, we did our best to get out and truly be a part of the city.

We weren't Indianapolis natives, but Indy was home. We were going to raise our children here and put down roots and embrace the fact that we were true Midwesterners living in a truly Midwestern city.

But then Jeff got transferred to Fort Wayne. Then five years later, after two exceptionally long, cold winters, we felt restless and ready to try something different. We turned our family's life upside down and headed to Texas.

For six years, we happily lived in the fourth largest city in the country, a city full of transplants from all over the world where we believed we could put down roots and live forever. Our Indiana kids—our daughter born in Indianapolis and our son born in Fort Wayne—started to see themselves as Texans; they accepted the heat and humidity and embraced year-round shorts-wearing and swimming in our backyard as a natural part of their lives.

But something in me never stopped longing for Indianapolis. Every time I saw a Colts game and the city skyline behind Lucas Oil Stadium. Every time we watched a sporting event that presented a shot of Monument Circle. Every time a former student or a friend or my sister posted pictures on social media of places all over the city. Every time I turned on HGTV and it was running another episode of the Indianapolis-based *Good Bones*. Every time I saw any of it—I felt a little pang from knowing that we were so far away and that the place we had thought would be our forever home would never be home again.

When I lost my job in early 2021, something in me snapped. I needed to go "home." I needed to be closer to family again. I needed to be around old friends who I knew would stand by us no matter what. I needed to be back in the familiar Midwest because, as much as I didn't want to admit it, I was a Midwestern girl through and through and that was where our family needed to be.

So we found a way. I found a new job and my work-from-home husband willingly pivoted to a new and different home office. We bought a house just outside the city so we could enjoy country living and still take advantage of everything Indy had to offer. We were away for eleven years and yet sometimes it feels like we never left. I found another new job and started teaching in the same district our kids would have attended school had we never moved. We occasionally return to our favorite Chinese take-out place and repeatedly ask ourselves why we didn't go certain places more often. Everything feels familiar and comfortable in a way I didn't anticipate, no matter how much I wanted to return.

In our first year back in the city, we got a year-long zoo membership and visited in every season. We've attended football games and Final Fours at Lucas Oil. We witnessed the changing of seasons in our favorite Indiana state parks. In the unexpected twists and turns of life, we somehow found ourselves coming full circle back to the Circle City.

We're back where we were always meant to be.

Midwestern Girl

I ALWAYS PRIDED MYSELF on being a California baby. Not just a California baby, but a blond-haired, blue-eyed Southern California baby born to return to her homeland. When I was nine, my parents somehow scraped enough money together for our family to fly to California to visit some of their friends from the two years they had lived there. We explored Disneyland, visited the animals at the San Diego Zoo, and drove through the campus at Concordia College, Irvine, where I decided I was destined to be a college student so that I could become the California girl I knew I had always been destined to be.

But I wasn't a California girl. I was a Midwestern girl masquerading as a girl from the Pacific Coast because I thought that was somehow more interesting than the girl I really was. The Midwest wasn't just something I inherited from my parents; it was a big part of my own lived experience.

Summers cooling off in Lake St. Clair and occasional dips in the Great Lakes taught me that freshwater was far superior to saltwater. I'm significantly better at building a snowman than I ever would be at riding a surfboard. I lived in Detroit for longer than I've lived anywhere else, and that is where most of my sports loyalties lie. And I love the change of the seasons.

Despite living in Wyoming for five years of my adolescence, the rest of my life has been consistently influenced by the Midwest. My parents and sisters and I lived in Michigan and Illinois, and then when I got married, my Michigan-raised husband and I moved to Indiana, where we lived for thirteen years before our move to Texas. Even my years going to college in eastern

Nebraska, technically part of the Great Plains, were colored by the Midwest. Most of my friends were from the Midwest. I traveled back and forth across the 600 miles with a car full of Michigan people. When I spent a semester in London, I was surrounded by people from all over the central portion of the United States. Most of us called the Midwest home, and when we returned and eventually graduated, many of us would continue to make it where we raised our families.

When Jeff and I made the decision to move to Texas, it wasn't a decision we took lightly. We knew it would be a significant change for us and our kids, but at the time it was what we needed. It wasn't that we needed to escape the Midwest, but life had gotten to the point where we felt we needed a drastic change that would enrich our lives. And it did. We learned what good Tex-Mex *really* tastes like, we traveled across the south and saw natural beauty and historical landmarks that we never would have experienced if we had stayed in Indiana, and we met wonderful people who became good friends who stuck with us to the bitter end. We gained a greater understanding of our country's complex racial history and learned just how devastating a hurricane can actually be. We fell in love with a place and the people who made that place home.

But the truth is I was never going to be okay with carved pumpkins that started rotting less than 24 hours after being put outside. I was never going to be okay with never again putting up a fresh blue spruce in my house at Christmas. I was never going to be okay with the fact that my kids got up every morning to say a pledge to the state of Texas. I was never going to be okay with both of them asking for huge and expensive mums and garters for Homecoming Week. I was never going to be okay with the dread that every hurricane season brought, wondering if we would make it through another season relatively unscathed. I was honestly never going to be okay with the deeply unapologetic devotion to a state and the tunnel vision that it created in otherwise lovely people and good friends.

Texas will always be, for my kids, what the American West has always been for me. It is a deep part of them. It will call them back, maybe not to live, but certainly to visit. The five years that my parents and sisters and I spent living in Wyoming instilled a deep love for mountains and canyons and an appreciation for desert-dry air in the middle of summer. The six years that we spent living in Texas gave my kids a deep love for the biodiversity of the second largest state in the United States and an appreciation for being able to swim in their outdoor pool and wear shorts year-round.

But because we took the Midwest with us to Texas, it is still very much a part of who they are. We raised them University of Michigan and Colts fans because our geographic location wasn't going to change our loyalty. We taught them that the only way to properly prepare brats was in a large pan full of boiling beer. We continued to fight against the urge to call carbonated beverages "soda" by insisting that, in our house, they were still called "pop."

And just as five years living in Wyoming enriched my life and made me a more well-rounded individual, my children will be able to say the same about Texas.

A return to Indianapolis meant a return to a region that was really home.

And while I was not ready to be called outside to help with the collection of what seems to be a metric ton of fallen leaves, I *was* ready for the fall colors and the smell of the leaves as they crunch underneath my feet. While I was not ready for winter, for bone-chilling cold that takes my breath away and a long driveway with impassable snow drifts, I *was* ready for that first snowfall that blankets the earth in a pure white, covering the dried and dead grass and leaves underneath. While I was not ready for the false spring that pretends to appear after a late snowfall and convinces me that winter has officially passed, I *was* ready for a spring that doesn't cover my car in yellow tree pollen and the budding of flowers that come up from the ground after a winter of death and decay.

Because I'm finally ready to admit that I'm a Midwestern girl. I may have wandered, but wandering makes us richer and helps us appreciate even the most mundane elements of home.

And we are *home*.

Motherhood

Death of Toe Shoe Dreams

I DREAMED OF BECOMING a prima ballerina. I danced all the time. I danced in my dreams. I walked on my toes. When my dad played his guitar, I donned a leotard and tutu and danced for my living room audience, occasionally turning his guitar case or the fireplace hearth into my stage.

I read books about ballerinas, watched every movie and show I could that had dancing in it, and at one point, had a calendar full of pointe shoes.

But ballet is expensive, and my dad worked for a church and my mom stayed at home. The dance classes alone would have bankrupted my family. And so I passed from childhood to adolescence to young adulthood with an unfulfilled dream, a dream that wasn't helped when a friend, who was a dancer, told me during my senior year of high school that I had perfect arches for toe shoes.

That settled it. Forget the fact that I had strong but short and thick legs and a less-than-lithe frame, my perfectly formed arches had been wasted on years of piano and short athletic careers in basketball, softball, and track. I decided then and there that if I ever had a daughter, I would make sure she got to take dance lessons for as long as she wanted.

We were blessed with a tall, beautiful, not-quite-graceful little girl. I knew from years of reading fictional stories about dancing that if she was going to be a dancer, we needed to start early, so when she was four I decided to try ballet at the YMCA close to our house. While she enjoyed the once-a-week classes, she didn't fall in love with it as I had hoped. When we gave her the choice of playing basketball or taking dance again after Christmas break, she chose basketball. To this day I'm not quite sure why we even gave her a choice. She was four and had no idea what she was really interested in, but we were trying to be good Xennial parents and wanted to make sure our kids had a variety of experiences.[1]

It was a disaster. First, they gave all of the kids colored bracelets to help them identify which kid on the other team they were supposed to guard. She thought that meant that she was supposed to become their best friend and kept trying to hold her opponent's hand. Then, she would get bored with the action on the court and wander away from the action so that she could dance around on her toes. By the time the season was over, I had signed her up for another creative dance class close to our house and decided that was where we were going to expend her physical energy.

The next year I signed her up for ballet through the dance studio that was hosted out of our church. When one of the after-school programs at her school offered a weekly hip-hop class, I signed her up for that one as well. I figured if she had to wait after school for me to be done with my teaching duties, she might as well be doing something active. She loved both her "beautiful" dance and her "cool" dance (her words, not ours), but by the performance dates for both studios, it was clear to us that dancing, no matter how much she enjoyed it, was not one of her natural gifts.

With our lives in total disarray during the first couple months after we moved to Houston, I wasn't signing our kids up for any extra activities. We didn't have a house yet, and we didn't know where anything was located. In fact, we were barely surviving

---

1. As someone born in 1979, I've come to appreciate the description of my microgeneration as Xennials, the Oregon Trail Generation. We don't quite fit Gen X or Millennials for a variety of reasons. We were children of the 80s who spent our entire teen years in the 90s. I think it's a pretty apt description.

the day-to-day as we juggled work, school, and life in a 30-foot travel trailer designed for weekend camping, not for living.

The following fall I once again asked our daughter if she wanted to take dance, but it appeared that any desire she had to take dance classes had dissipated. Disappointed, I was also woman enough to admit I was not "dance mom" material. I wasn't girly enough to hang out with the other dance moms, crafty enough to help with costumes, or patient enough to twist my daughter's thick, yet fine, long hair into a tight, perfectly formed bun for every dance rehearsal.

The following spring, as I was asking our son if he wanted to play soccer, our daughter jumped right on it.

"I want to play."

"Really?" I tried to keep the surprise out of my voice—because I never wanted to give my daughter the impression that she couldn't do anything her brother could do—but I couldn't help remembering back to our experience with basketball three years before. I wasn't sure I was ready for a repeat performance.

But we weren't going to tell our son he could play soccer and tell our daughter "no" for no reason other than sports had been a miserable failure when she was in preschool. So we signed both kids up for spring soccer, and, much to our surprise, she not only loved playing the game that had terrified me in Freshman P.E. (I hated people kicking at my shins), but her favorite position was goalie. Our daughter, who screamed every time I discovered a tiny knot in her long hair, enjoyed having soccer balls kicked *at* her.

Will wonders never cease.

Then she discovered basketball after we signed her up against her will. She discovered that she didn't need anyone to play with if she wanted to shoot baskets. If she wanted to practice goalkeeping she needed a partner to shoot balls in her direction, but shooting hoops was something she could do without additional assistance.

She enjoyed playing sports, and I had to do deep soul-searching to finally admit that the toe shoe dreams were about me, not her.

And while the dream of my little girl achieving *my* dreams may continue to go unfulfilled, it is just one of many dreams I have for my daughter. I also wanted her to love sports, and she picked two sports that we enjoyed watching her play for several years. She loves Harry Potter nearly as much as I do, and I treasure the moments that we have shared reading many different books together, even though she has been able to read on her own for years. We still share a common love of music and dance and drama, as evidenced by our occasional moments breaking out into singing along to Broadway cast recordings and now her desire to do theater in school. And I did eventually fulfill my promise to take her to a production of *The Nutcracker*, because while she's past the years of dance lessons, she still appreciates the beauty of the art form.

Sometimes as parents it's hard to let go of our dreams and let our kids pursue their own, but like so many of my parenting peers, I'm learning.

But that doesn't mean I'm going to stop spinning on my own toes.

Our Dreams Are Not Theirs

I STARTED PLAYING PIANO when I was in second grade. Looking back, I don't know that I really had much of a choice, at least at the beginning. My mom served as our church organist, we had a piano in our Detroit basement, and music was how our family entertained ourselves. We would either listen to our mom play piano downstairs, singing along when we knew the words, or we would sing and dance upstairs in the living room while my dad played his guitar for us. Some of my earliest memories are of me dancing on his guitar case or standing around the piano at my grandparents' home in Ontario, singing along with the rest of my dad's family when everyone was home.

Music was a way of life. I pounded on the piano keys from the time I could reach them, and it was only natural to want to learn what those signs in front of my mom meant.

Then my mother became my piano teacher.

At least she tried. I thought the progress was too slow, and I didn't like listening to her directions. I also didn't want to practice. But we didn't have money to spare, so if I was going to learn to play piano, I had to suck it up and accept lessons at home. And there was no way she was going to let me quit. Her oldest daughter was going to learn how to play piano, period.

My mom went on to start all four of us girls on the piano, but eventually she moved us on to "real" teachers. Not that she wasn't a real teacher. She took on her first piano student shortly after she started teaching me. But when it came to her daughters, we all eventually needed to be moved to the care of someone we didn't live with. Under the tutelage of my new piano teacher, I thrived throughout my middle school and early high school years. I played recitals, participated in a duet concert, and eventually accompanied my high school choir on at least one number per concert. I enjoyed playing and appreciated the opportunities that my teacher gave me.

However, I eventually stopped playing. I never intended to, but the later years of high school got busy, college got even busier, and then I was struggling to keep my head above water as a new teacher. It wasn't that I didn't enjoy running my fingers across the keys, but I found other tasks and hobbies that drew my attention. I can still read music and sit down to play simpler pieces, but I would rather write than play, and so that is what I do in my spare time.

Still, I determined that when we had children, they would learn how to play piano. Basic music skills are good for academics, creativity, and personal development. I want my children to be well-rounded, and that means a healthy mix of the arts and athletics.

So when our daughter announced at the age of six that she wanted to learn how to play the violin, I told her that she wasn't getting violin lessons until she learned the basics in piano. I dreamed of listening to her play on the keys and falling in love with the creation of music at her fingertips. I couldn't wait to make videos to send her piano teacher grandmother so that she could see her granddaughter's progress from a distance.

But as with my ballet dreams, reality frequently does not match our fantasies.

She enjoyed playing piano, but she didn't like the process. She didn't want to spend thirty minutes a day practicing. She didn't want to work on her theory books (which was also one of my biggest weaknesses). She didn't want to take the time to get better. She just wanted to get into piano lessons, hear what her teacher had to say, absorb about half of it, and then return home to whatever she was doing before we left for piano.

Frustrated and stubborn, I refused to give up.

I know I should probably have done so earlier, but I had dreams. I just knew that someday it would click, someday she would discover the benefits of practicing piano and she would take off. It never happened.

After we added the extra responsibility of middle school soccer to the mix of our family life, I asked her what she wanted to do about piano.

"Well, I don't want to play violin anymore, so I think I can quit."

To be honest, I was a little hurt. I asked if she was sure. She said that she was.

When my daughter decided she was done with dance, it was the end of my own unfulfilled childhood dreams. But when she said she was done with piano, it felt like so much more than that. It felt like a rejection of one of the things that had been such a big part of my own childhood.

But I know that's not fair. After all, she's never seen her mom lose herself in a piece of music, fingers flying up and down the ivories. Instead she's watched her mom spend hours lost in her own writing, her fingers making words instead of music. As a result, she has spent years developing her own writing, creating stories and drawing pictures to match, convinced that someday she will create something worthy of others' praise. Her stage is the page, not the baby grand.

My entire life I've heard older women lament the fact that they never learned to play piano or wishing that they had never stopped. Now that I'm older and I've experienced both learning to play and no longer doing so, I wonder if maybe the lament is because they never found something to fill that grand-piano-sized creative hole. I'm glad that I spent all of those years playing, but I also am okay with the fact that I don't play anymore.

Watching my daughter move into the more complicated sphere of middle school sports and fine arts while balancing school and practices and rehearsals and important friend and family time has convinced me that we don't need to add one more time-consuming activity into the mix. I don't need to keep fighting her on her practicing routine, looking over her shoulder to see if she's actually playing the right notes or just the notes she wants to play. She has fallen in love with choir, choosing to use her voice as her instrument instead of the piano or violin. I'm okay with that. I really am.

And I still have one more shot with my son, who has now taken on his father's instrument in beginner band. While I still have to remind him to practice his saxophone, the discovery of my long-forgotten guitar in a closet has convinced him to keep learning and playing, at least for a while. He wants to earn the right to make my old guitar his own, as long as he can put down whatever ball or game controller he has in his hands long enough to sit down and make some music.

I have to keep hoping at least a little bit, don't I?

When Mommy Gets Sick

H1N1 MADE ITS UGLY appearance the fall after we brought our daughter home from the hospital. I made it my yearly mission to get whatever flu vaccine was available, but those precautions didn't prevent Jeff from eventually coming home with the flu bug that ravaged the country. He kept arguing that he didn't have it and that he was going to be fine, but his illness ran the course that every other H1N1 case ran: high fever, apparent wellness, and then the return of fever, chills, and general achiness and weakness.

I wasn't taking any chances with our baby girl. I sprayed every surface, repeatedly washed linens, and quarantined my dear husband to our bedroom, refusing to let him wander the house and following him with Lysol every time he had to leave our bedroom.

And while our baby daughter and I got through that particular epidemic unscathed, I have not been impervious to illnesses over the years.

Oh, colds and coughs are kind of par for the course. Nearly every year of our marriage I have lost my voice at some point, although our move to Texas unexpectedly lowered the instances of laryngitis. But every once in a while, no matter how many precautions I take (I am a faithful yearly recipient of the flu vaccine and now the COVID booster), I succumb to an illness that sends me straight to bed, kicking and screaming and making bold claims that I'm a mom and a teacher and I don't have time for this nonsense.

When viruses knock on our doors, they don't care if we have kids who need to be fed and homework that needs to be checked and practices and games that need to be attended and kids that need to be rushed off to bed at a decent hour. The nasty bugs attack our sleep-deprived immune systems and attempt to knock us out of the parenting ring. And these viral attacks are bad enough when we have a partner to swoop in and pick up the slack. But what happens when we don't?

Several years ago, our daughter came home with a fever and the clear markers of the flu. It was the middle of the week and we had a couple of days before my sister and brother-in-law would be coming down for a visit, so as soon as I was home from school and had evaluated the situation, I decided we needed illness confirmation. Sure enough, she had Influenza A. Since Jeff usually works from home, she got to spend the next three days moving between the couch and her bed while my son and I kept going to school. She eventually felt well enough to hang out with the rest of the family, including my sister and brother-in-law once they arrived from Idaho.

After years of living with a global pandemic that keeps disrupting our lives with new variants and waves, my behavior in the days following her illness still feel less than sufficient. I cleaned, I washed sheets and bedding, I ran the air purifiers, but I still nervously waited for the other shoe to drop. Jeff's next business trip was only days away, and I was certain that our son was going to be the next one to fall and that I would have to take time off of work to stay home with him.

But instead of my son, it was *my* sleep-deprived body that succumbed to the flu.

By the time I admitted I had a problem and told the school office to take my temperature on Monday morning, Jeff was packing up to leave for a four-day business trip. It was Monday morning. He wasn't going to be home until Thursday night. I clearly didn't have time to be sick, but my body didn't care.

When I got home from picking up the kids from school, I told them to get themselves snacks and work on their homework. Could they play video games? Sure. I didn't care. I was going back to bed. Thankfully, at seven and nine, they were finally to the age where they could be left alone to their own devices in small spurts, especially since I was just upstairs resting and keeping myself quarantined from the kids and my still-visiting sister and brother-in-law. With the significant help of my baby sister, who didn't leave until early Tuesday morning, our daughter still made it to her evening basketball practice and the kids got fed, even if it was pizza.

Since my sister and her husband left *early* on Tuesday, I really was on my own for the whole day. And it didn't matter that I had been in bed by 9:30 P.M., I felt like I deserved a trophy just for getting the kids to school on time. I spent the day traveling back and forth between the couch and my bed, finding enough energy early in the day to work on some grading and responding to students and finally giving up before noon, trading my laptop for a bath and more sleep. I convinced myself that I didn't need to be a hero, that energy needed to be reserved for that night.

You see, the week my body decided to get the flu at the same time as my husband was gone wasn't just *any* week. It was the first week of a three-week overlap of basketball and soccer practices for both kids and the week that they had elementary school halftime performances for their P.E. basketball skills unit. Tuesday was a trifecta of two TOTs (Teams of Tomorrow) performances and one soccer practice, all back-to-back. And yes, common sense would say "just drop events" or "ask someone for help" or "pretend you forgot that any of those events ever existed and hide at home," but since when does parenting make sense? Missing the first soccer practice of the season was going to put our daughter behind on gelling with a new group of girls, and even if I had gotten someone to take my kids to their TOTs performances, I actually wanted to watch them, so *I* would be missing out. Besides, my fever had broken in the morning, so I was finding every reason to justify my desire to be super mom.

Remember how I said this was a pre-COVID world with pre-COVID expectations of doing it all no matter how we feel?

I just did it, even if my body still felt like the very life was being sucked from it. I was miserable and dragging and didn't have very many nice replies to their every question and concern, but I watched both performances from an isolated spot in the balcony of the gym and stayed in the car during the duration of my daughter's soccer practice. By the time I dragged my exhausted body into bed, I wondered how we would keep this up for another two days.

By day three, twenty-four hours after my fever returned to normal range, I dragged the kids to school and myself back to work. I took it easy, or, at least, I tried. By the time a couple of students took short make-up quizzes after school and I was headed to pick up both of our kids, I was exhausted. Not "I feel like I'm going to die because I'm so sick" exhausted, but "My body just needs to sit and do nothing for the rest of the night" exhausted. But valentines hadn't been purchased for Friday parties and Thursday night was booked with a soccer and basketball practice (let's hear it again for a three-week sports overlap!) so we needed to get them *now*.

We got home; I instructed the kids to empty the dishwasher, make their lunches, and get started on their valentines. If they needed me, I would be lying down for half an hour.

Twenty minutes later: "Mommy, I need you! Mom, I need your help."

Oh, for the LOVE.

I came downstairs to both kids dutifully doing what they were asked. The dishwasher was emptied, their lunches packed and in the fridge, and their valentines were strewn in front of them on the not-quite-clean table.

My first-grade son, ever concerned about making sure he spelled all of his friends' names correctly, asked if I had a list. After twenty minutes of horizontal rest, I was finally able to think clearly enough to hand him the class list which I had carefully pinned to the bulletin board the very weekend we had gotten the note from his teacher. Then I noticed a sticky substance on some of the cards.

"Wait, did you check to see if the table was clean first???" I had to take a deep breath. After all, I was still recovering from the flu, and he had taken it upon himself to make sure his valentines were done. He had carefully selected them and written names on each one. Who cared if he had cut them apart instead of using the perforated lines to tear them apart? Or that he had taken the plastic cover off of all of the tattoos? My little boy was exerting independence and taking care of things instead of depending on his sick mom. That had to be worth something, right?

By the time Jeff got home Thursday night and we figured out the balance of getting our son to two practices and dinner into everyone's bodies, I was at the end of my rope. When my loving husband asked if he could go play basketball (at the time, his one social recreational activity outside of working from home), I almost lost it.

My head is stuffy and we have beds that need to be changed to prevent further spread of illness and the house is a mess and I haven't gotten anything done for work all week and the kids need to go to bed at a decent hour and don't you know that I just want to be spoiled and I don't care how but for the love of everything holy it is Valentine's Day and I don't care that we don't normally celebrate but I deserve something!

Of course, I kept all of those thoughts to myself. I just didn't have the energy left to explain to anyone that I didn't have the energy to deal.

When he apologetically walked into the door several hours later he held a bouquet of flowers. Not a "hey there Valentine, wink, wink" bouquet of flowers but a "I know that we don't do this sort of thing and I don't normally get you flowers but you really deserve it after the last week" bouquet of flowers.

Yeah, I forgave him.

When we're parents, illness is often the unexpected curveball that derails us in many ways. While we plan for the moments when our kids may get short-term illnesses (and dread the possibility that our kids will get long-term illnesses that test our emotional and spiritual resolve), *we* aren't supposed to be the ones to get sick. We're supposed to be the strong ones, changing linens and cleaning up bathrooms and checking temperatures while still keeping the rest of the family functioning. It is so hard to accept when we no longer have control of any of the above and we have to take care of ourselves instead. And our kids expect us to be invincible, as well. My kids didn't know what to do with one parent gone and one down for the count. They weren't used to me being the one sick and in need of care. They didn't know how to respond when I yelled at them that I didn't know or that I just needed them to take care of it themselves.

But we have to give ourselves grace too. My kids were fine. They were still fed. They still got their homework done. Their classmates all got carefully addressed valentines. They still got to their events. Having a little extra time on *Madden* and *Minecraft* during a single week wasn't going to hurt them. And I had to learn to accept help as well. I don't know what I would have done that first day of the flu if it hadn't been for my sister and brother-in-law, and on Wednesday, after a full day of working, I was relieved when I ran into a friend while picking up the kids who insisted that I let her take the kids back to church for their scheduled Grow Groups. It was time resting that I didn't know I needed until I got up from two hours of vegging on the couch and realized I felt like a new woman. But even if I hadn't swallowed my pride and accepted the help of others, we would have survived; we just would have had to make harder choices.

We all survived my short bout of flu. And a few years later we survived my days of COVID quarantine when it finally caught up with me. And we'll survive the next time I get knocked down for more than a day.

Sometimes we moms need to be reminded that it isn't all on us. Sometimes our children and spouses need that reminder as well. We all just have to remember to give each other a little more grace.

I Don't Miss the Early Years

I THINK NEARLY EVERY mother has had the same experience while they are holding their infant children in their arms: a well-meaning relative or older woman approaches them and says, "Treasure these moments. Someday you are going to miss it."

These words of wisdom are meant to be encouraging to exhausted mothers who can barely keep their eyes open while they are simultaneously questioning every decision they make concerning their baby and any other children they might be responsible for raising to adulthood. But if we're being honest, in that moment most mothers are just thinking about survival, not the distant future when they will miss holding their little bundle of joy.

I heard those words several times when both of my children were infants and toddlers. I understand why I was being told to treasure those moments, and I appreciate the sentiment. It only lasts for a short period of time. One minute you are snuggling a sleeping baby, the newborn smell reminding you why you wanted a baby in the first place. You blink, and they ride off alone on a bike, exerting independence and demonstrating just one more way they no longer need you.

There were things I loved about my babies. I loved playing with their little fingers and toes and watching them make new, daily discoveries. I loved holding their tiny bodies in my arms, knowing I could keep them safe there, even if it was only for a little while. I loved watching first steps and growing language skills and the reckless abandon that characterized their playtime as they devised games without any concern about what other people thought.

I loved all of those things about my own children's early childhood, but I don't miss it.

And maybe it's just me. I went into high school education for a reason, and not just because I like to read and write and discuss young adult and adult literature and the process of writing. If I'm being perfectly honest, little humans scare me. One summer, long before having children, I volunteered for our church's Vacation Bible School. My sister and I were put in charge of the story presentations. We presented to different age groups all morning long. My comfort steadily decreased as each group got younger and younger.

When the kindergarteners finally came in, I nearly lost my mind. The same thing was true several years later when we foolishly decided to host a birthday party for our daughter's sixth birthday. We invited fifteen five and six-year-olds to a science museum and had to keep track of all of them as they ran around exploring the hands-on exhibits. My deep respect for early childhood educators grew as I tried to manage a crew of inquisitive little people intent on wandering off towards anything that caught their eyes. I was overwhelmed by the energy it took to keep all of them focused on one task.

Despite these personal failings when it comes to other people's small children, I've never had a problem with my own little humans. I've loved watching my kids grow through every stage of their lives so far. I remember dreading the "terrible twos" only to discover that two was *so* much fun. Our kids started speaking and expressing and developing personalities and it only made me look forward to the people they were going to grow up to be. I loved their snuggles and giggles and inexplicable joy at the little things. I see memories pop up in my Facebook feed and my heart overflows with joy at the beautiful parenting moments our family has shared together.

But there is *so* much about those early years that I just do not miss.

Lost sleep, diapers, bottles, food messes, spit-up, carrying increasingly heavier babies around, strollers (although I *do* sometimes miss having the excuse of a stroller for carrying supplies when we're someplace like the zoo), baby carriers, inexplicable crying with no way to verbally communicate what is wrong, fighting flailing limbs as we try to get clothes onto them, the loss of lazy Saturday mornings, the inability to focus in church, and the list goes on.

I once read a blog post about the sweet spot of parenting.[1] At the time it felt like we were still years away from that ever being us, but the post gave me hope. It wasn't that I wasn't enjoying watching our kids grow up. I've loved every new stage, each with a new perspective and insight into the people our children are growing up to be. As our kids have moved from one stage to the next, I've tried to embrace the new and, sometimes begrudgingly, let go of the previous stage. When old pictures of chubby cheeks and gleeful smiles pop up, I sigh, sniffle, and then happily remember the digitally captured moments before moving on to the here and now.

But we did arrive in the elusive sweet spot. Because our kids are only two years apart, they arrived in that late elementary age of growing independence in quick succession. During the week they pick out their own clothes and dress themselves (with occasional corrections when the clothes don't match the outside temperatures or fit into school dress codes). On Saturday mornings our kids can get their own breakfast and turn on what they want to watch (and 99% of the time they make good choices). When we still lived in Texas, they could jump into the pool and they didn't need further assistance, just supervision. They can play in the backyard and play basketball in our driveway and they don't need help. It took too long, but we felt victorious when both of our kids finally got off of training wheels, allowing for

---

1. Miner, Julianna W. "The Sweet Spot of Parenthood Exists, I'm in It Right Now." *Scary Mommy*, 26 August 2019, https://www.scarymommy.com/the-sweet-spot. Accessed 12 October 2022.

easier family bike rides and freedom to ride to places close enough to home without our supervision. They can make macaroni and cheese and quesadillas and our son gladly makes himself peanut butter sandwiches when the hunger hits. They read to themselves and now we occasionally have full family read-ins. They are fully capable of helping with chores and taking responsibility for keeping our family and home fully functioning. They are realizing and slowly exerting their independence but still fully enjoy being together as a family. In short, they don't usually hate us, even as we approach both of them entering adolescence.

No matter the stage, being a parent is still work. Each phase just brings a different kind of work, and with each phase of parenthood we have tried to embrace how our roles have changed. And even though being a parent at every stage is still hard work, I'm loving the humans they are growing into.

Family camping trips have become increasingly fun as the kids jump in to help with setting up camp and beg to play intellectually challenging games; we can also go on hikes and bike rides without baby carriers and tow-behind trailers. My daughter wants to snuggle in her bed and have deep conversations about life, the world, and growing up, and she at least pretends to believe that I'm an authority in all of those things.

No, there is a lot about the baby and toddler years that I do not miss, but as my children now move into adolescence, you know what I do miss?

I miss snuggling up under a blanket to read bedtime stories. I miss watching them create entire worlds with their stuffed animals and other toys. I miss ridiculous explanations for rocket ships powered by the sun and how it is going to be an engineering feat that is going to make my son rich. I actually miss little kid soccer and basketball games where the kids are showing growth in skill but the competition hasn't yet become cutthroat. I miss their desire to be with us more than with their friends. And because it hasn't happened yet, I'm going to miss ready hugs and hearing "Mom, I love you," with no strings attached.

We have now reached puberty and pre-adolescence. I miss parenting before hormones and changing bodies complicated their lives and ours. I miss how simple and idyllic life seemed before we decided to move our kids across the country while their bodies and emotions and life perspectives were also changing.

But even there we've had pleasant surprises. I did not look forward to re-living my own painfully awkward adolescence and attempting to wisely guide my little girl through it. And while our move was a particularly difficult struggle for her and us, we've kept communication open enough that she still comes to us for occasional words of wisdom. I did not look forward to a return to nonsensical mood swings. But we've also spent a lot of time trying to prepare our kids for the biological changes ahead. I did not look forward to trying to advise through the inevitable middle school fights with friends. But when we faced our most difficult situations so far, we consistently reminded our kids that we loved them and would help see them through. I'm still not looking forward to crushes and boyfriends and girlfriends and trying to help them wisely navigate a dangerous combination of strong emotions and confusing hormones. But as long as they keep talking to us, we think we might get through that too.

Despite the challenges at our doorstep, I am still confident in saying that I don't miss those early years and I have no desire to go back. Instead, I plan to live in the moment that we have and do our best to embrace the moments yet to come.

And as parents, that's the best that we can do.

More Than a Mother

I AM A MOTHER.

I remember the first time the weight of that identification hit me with its full force. It was shortly after my daughter was born. I got a phone call from the pediatrician's office for her first infant well-check.

When I picked up the phone, the question wasn't, "Is Sarah there?" It was, "Is this L's mother?"[1]

There was pride and joy in answering that question, because I was holding my long-awaited-for child in my arms. My desire for a baby was finally fulfilled. Her presence filled a hole in my heart, and I knew that, while there would be heartache in my love for this little one, she was still mine to love and care for over the next eighteen years and beyond.

I was so excited to be a mother. I couldn't wait to finally be called "Mommy." But I kept fighting to ensure that the title of "Mommy" wouldn't absorb my whole identity.

And we live in a culture that loves to use our relationship to others to form our identities.

It starts with the many holidays that we celebrate. For me, nowhere is this truer than with Mother's Day. To be honest, Mother's Day has raised a lot of complicated feelings for me throughout my adulthood. I've always wanted to honor my own

---

1. Several years ago I decided to give my children as much anonymity as they wanted when it came to my writing. I'm sure that someday they'll give me permission to use their full names, but until then, I'm respecting their privacy.

mother. But as I approached 30 and was still childless, Mother's Day became a painful reminder that it wasn't a day to celebrate me. I finally celebrated my first Mother's Day, as a mother, one month before my thirtieth birthday. But as much as I rejoiced in the expansion of my family, I never forgot the emotional and spiritual pain of watching other women celebrate a holiday in which I could not participate.

Motherhood has always been complicated. The Bible is full of women who lived their lives childless or grieved the loss of children, either by death or broken relationship. But we find that the state of their motherhood or lack thereof did not ultimately define them. God still used them and made it clear that He did not determine their value by the productivity of their wombs. Miriam stood by her brothers in ministry through exile and led the Jewish people in praising God, but we are never told whether she had children. Esther saved the Jewish people through her patience and cunning and is never defined by motherhood. Naomi found new life in her relationship with her daughter-in-law and helped her find a new husband, securing their social position. Mary and Martha of Bethany are seen as important early followers of Jesus, yet we never know if they were married and had children. Mary Magdalene is never identified as a wife or a mother, and yet she is the first woman to see Jesus alive after the resurrection and proclaim the risen Lord to his disciples.

Motherhood is an incredible gift and essential to the peopling of the planet, but it isn't the only reason God created women.

God didn't create me to make babies. He created me for so much more than that.

Yes, being a mother was one of my deepest desires. Having a family to love and nurture was one of the many goals I set for myself as a child and young adult. But I also discovered a love for teaching and education and activism and ministry and everything in-between. My children don't see me as "just" their mom I am more than someone who wipes their tears and gives them hugs and reads to them at night. They see me outside of that role all while embodying that role, and they take great pride in that.

And this is as it should be.

There is nothing wrong with motherhood. There is nothing wrong with celebrating the women who have given us life, nurtured us, and prepared us for adulthood. This is a celebration and commemoration that should happen all year long.

But women were built for so much more than that.

I know women who have only ever wanted to be mothers. They have dedicated their lives to the creation of strong and tightly knit families and have thrived in their roles as caretakers. This is not a burden to them but a blessing, and that should be celebrated.

I know women who have felt the ache of an empty womb and have filled it with love for other mothers' children, loving them in every way that they can. Whether single and childless or married with a committed partner in a union that could never produce children, they have faithfully served others, proving that it really does take a village to raise a child, and that should be celebrated.

I know women who have no desire to have children. Whether single or married, they feel a calling to serve their world in other ways. They are passionate and dedicated to their work. They aren't selling themselves short or missing out on having a family or grieving an empty womb; they are leaving the building of strong families to other women who they feel are better called to love and nurture children to adulthood.

And all of that is okay, because God built us for more than motherhood.

He created women with unique skills and emotional capacities that are not just suited to motherhood. He created us to live in community and serve each other, not just our families. He created us to be interdependent, not focused inward. He created us to be significant pieces in the bigger puzzle that is our earthly home.

I love being a mother and can't imagine my life as anything else, but I also believe that we should recognize that motherhood is not the primary task assigned to us at birth. I want to raise children who love Jesus, who understand that serving Jesus requires that they "do justly, love mercy, and walk humbly" in their acts of service to their fellow human beings and the planet we call home.[2] And I cannot do that alone. I depend on the other women in my life and the lives of my children.

For those of us blessed with children, we never stop being mothers. We never stop nurturing our children's mental, emotional, and spiritual needs. We also never stop risking mental, emotional, and spiritual harm to our children, no matter how inadvertent. Many of our life decisions for at least the first eighteen years of their lives are made prioritizing their needs over our own.

But we are so much more.

I don't want my daughter to believe that having children and blessing us with grandchildren is the most important achievement of her life. I want my son and daughter to both see the role of women as complex and significant to more than just making and raising babies.

Motherhood will always be one of the greatest joys in my life, because I pray that it will continue to offer a fullness far beyond the moment my children are officially grown. But it is not the only joy in my life nor is it the only vocation God has called me to.

Because *He* made me for so much more than that.

---

2. I've come to see Micah 6:8 as the best way to live my life as a Christian and as a citizen and I want my children to see their fellow human beings the same way.

Raising Good Humans

OUR SON CAME HOME, handed me a sheet of paper, and then turned to sit on the couch, making himself as small as possible.

"What's this?"

"Read it," Jeff responded as he walked up behind me.

Our son, who gets upset when he hears us say "darn" or "hell," regardless of the context, had gotten in trouble for telling a classmate to say the gold standard of profanities.

As it usually turns out, the story was way more complicated than the simple explanation on the piece of paper, but after getting clarification and apologizing to the friend's mother, we were still left with a despondent little boy. It wasn't just that he had gotten into trouble. He was convinced that his inexplicable slip-up meant he was a bad kid and he didn't deserve our love anymore.

Thankfully, a lot of discussion and hugs later, he finally believed that he was neither a bad kid nor undeserving of his parents' unconditional love. He had been reassured that he was a forgiven child of God and there was nothing he could do to change that.

The whole situation once again forced me to take careful stock of the kind of children that I want to raise and what matters most to me as they grow towards adulthood.

We are imperfect human beings raising smaller imperfect human beings who will face the same temptations we experienced as children. My children are kind, loving, and generous. They love each other and their parents, and they are the same towards their peers. But they are far from perfect. They can go from calmly playing a video game together to slamming doors in seconds.

They yell at us, forget to finish chores, and lie to get out of trouble. We are well aware that this is just the beginning. We have started the teen years and can see the sweet spot of parenting slipping between our fingers. We know this is the calm before the storm and all we can do is pray and hold on.

Most parents spend the first eighteen years of their child's life just hoping that they won't screw up. As a society, we measure how we are doing by comparing ourselves to other families. We look at the behavior of children of all ages and often say "at least we're not them." We see the news stories and ask what those parents did wrong to have their children turn out "that way."

But here's the thing: In the end, I'll know I was successful if I can be certain that I am sending genuinely good people out to live their lives. I'll know that I did my job well if I send out children who do not just profess that they are Christians but love and treat others as Jesus would. I'll know we were good and faithful servants if our children leave our home ready to use their natural gifts and privilege to change their world.

Would I love to see my children find tremendous personal and financial success at whatever path they choose in life?

Of course.

But for me, success isn't about the money in their pocket, the level of employment, or the size of their house. Those are all good things that will make their lives better and ease our parental worries once they are out of our home. But if they lack love and empathy for their fellow man, I have failed. If they ignore the needs of others, or, worse, gain success at the expense of those around them, I have failed. I want them to see the interconnected nature of life on earth so that they work to improve the lives of their weakest neighbors.

When our son came home with the note, I have to admit that one of my first thoughts was "what does his teacher think of us?" Our kids were attending a Christian school run by our church and associated with the Christian high school where I taught. I was afraid that this one incident would reflect on us as parents or Christians or even me as a teacher.

But he's also a kid, a kid who is learning and inquisitive and exploring the world around him. Part of that exploration, for better or worse, involves language. As he gets older, that world will also include other temptations with stronger consequences for him and others. I know from experience and watching my own friends and siblings grow up that even "good" kids can get swept up into the allure of behaviors that challenge their upbringing.

By the time I reached adulthood, I had learned that morality is often not the same as goodness. I know some strictly moral people who are not good to other human beings, and I know some apparently immoral people who are kind, generous, and treat all people the same.

We all fall short. But I'm increasingly seeing people who claim moral superiority as evidence of their goodness while ignoring how that strict "morality" is hurting those around them. Do I want my children to hold onto morals that enrich their lives and are evidence of their Christian faith? Yes, but I don't want my children to use that morality against those who do not see the world the same way they do. Their witness of faith should come from how people see their heart, not in a quest for unachievable perfection.

I want my children to grow into mature adults who understand their identity as forgiven saints and use that identity to make their world a better place. Being good doesn't mean they are perfect, it just means they learn from their mistakes, accept the consequences, and do better. My prayer is that if this is how they view their role in the world, they will also know that their parents will forgive their mistakes as well, trusting that we will love them unconditionally so they can come to us with any troubles they might be having. I don't want them to be afraid that a moral slip-up will define the way we see them, because that is not how God sees them either.

I want my kids to see morality as following Jesus's example and not just acting as perfectly as possible. I want my kids to embrace the idea of "good trouble" and understand that doing the right thing isn't always considered the socially appropriate thing. I don't want them to believe that sacrificing for saying they are followers of Jesus is enough; I want them to be willing to sacrifice for being *like* Jesus. I want them to love mercy and walk humbly.

By any metric, that isn't easy. As parents we've made plenty of mistakes and we continue to see our children make their own mistakes, full of consequences. We've had a lot of conversations about being open and honest and putting all of our cards on the table. We are all works-in-progress, just hoping that our mistakes won't have too much of an impact on others.

Ultimately, I want to know that the children I send out into the world are focused on making it better, flaws and all. My prayer is that they know they are forgiven sinners working for the good of humanity, faithful servants until the end.

Raising Contributors

FOR OUR DAUGHTER, STARTING fifth grade came with a lot of new and exciting opportunities. She got to pick her first elective: choir. She got to start middle school team sports, which meant we no longer had to drag her to practices (of course, we also found ourselves traveling all over the Houston area and adding more games to our family's schedule). The work was more challenging and increasingly fulfilled her desire for more knowledge.

And six months before the world shut down for COVID, she got to decorate her locker for the first time.

While she was definitely looking forward to choir and playing sports with her school friends, she started obsessing over what she was going to do to decorate her locker the moment we returned from our family summer vacation.

I understood her excitement. That same school year I moved across the hall into a new classroom, and I couldn't wait to start decorating my own space. But my children have the misfortune of having a teacher mother who has seen all sorts of behavioral patterns from students over the years. After a decade and a half of watching high school students decorate and then throw away mounds of waste at the end of the year, I wasn't ready to jump on board with the whole "buy all the things to make the locker pretty" bandwagon.

When our daughter dragged me to Target to pick out her dream décor, I discovered just how much things had changed since I bought my first locker accessories twenty-five years before. Did you know that stores now sell beaded curtains to put just inside a locker door so that you have to pull aside beads *every* time you want to put something in or take something out? Neither did I, until I was forced to look at the costly and expansive display.

I gave her a budget, and she realized she didn't have nearly enough to buy everything she wanted because she wanted it *all*: the magnets, the shelf, the mirror and pencil holder. Then she picked up the *piece de resistance*: magnetic wallpaper to stick to the back of the locker.

"Mom, didn't you decorate your locker when you were my age?"

"Well I didn't get my first locker until I was in high school, but sure. Of course, I had to pay for all of it."

"You DID?!?!"

"Yep, are you sure you need all of those things?"

"Well *everyone* else is getting all sorts of stuff to decorate. Their moms are buying *everything*."

Sigh.

I slowly talked her away from the $30 magnetic wallpaper when I pointed out that no one was really going to see it and it was not just a waste of money, but a waste of ecological resources. When I asked her where it was going to end up when she was done with it, she sheepishly looked back at me and said, "A landfill."

Apparently, I had appealed to her sense of environmental justice. She could be satisfied with the other items which she could actually find use for.

I wish I could say this economics lesson stuck, but it hasn't. It feels like we have similar conversations with both of our children multiple times a year.

We parents want our kids to have everything we can possibly give them. When we can't afford "all the things" or even "most of the things," it can be emotionally crushing. We know that our kids are loved and we are doing our best to take care of their every need, but parents also have a strong desire to make sure that our kids have it better than we had it, even if that isn't feasible. And while this often comes out in the way we sign our kids up for every activity under the sun, we also see this when we walk into our kids' bedrooms and playrooms.

It doesn't stop after early childhood, either. One of the customs I found most jarring when we moved from the Midwest to Texas is the tradition of "Mums and Garters" for Homecoming. My first year in Houston I was shocked by the number of my students who came in with full-body-sized monstrosities of school color ribbons and trinkets, a sign of just how much their significant other (or more likely their significant other's mother) liked them. These mum and garters can cost upwards of $300 or more and serve as a constant distraction for an entire day as students struggle underneath the extra weight and bulk, often draping them over a spare spot in the classroom for the duration of a period of learning.

Several years ago, the school I taught at in Texas decided to suggest our students to forgo the purchase of mums and garters (or at least significantly downsize) and encourage them to donate towards our yearly Costa Rica house building project. While people gladly started donating to the building of a home, it took a couple of years before I saw a significant decrease in the size and number of mums and garters that were floating around our hallways. It was a refreshing change of pace. There were several students who held on tightly to the tradition, but the students almost seemed as relieved as we teachers that they didn't have to deal with the extra annoyance for an entire school day.

The realities of parenting in a consumer-driven society often leaves me feeling more than a little dizzy. And it's not like we're the best examples. Every time we move, we have multiple "why do we have this?" conversations. We usually walk away, shaking our heads and throwing multiple items in the trash or donation pile, trying to remember when we bought the item or even when we last used it. Each time we move into the next house, we repeat the process as we try to find a home for everything we unpack, realizing that we wasted space in the moving truck that could have been used for something we wish we had moved instead.

I just get so tired of all of the junk.

And I'm not saying that as parents we need to strip our children of the joy of marking an academic transition or completely ignore social traditions. And it can be really hard to feel like you're the only one who isn't caving to the pressure, especially when you remember how much it hurt to feel left out when it was you all those years ago (as is far too often the case for me).

I want better for my kids. I want them to find joy in people and experiences. I want to unburden our family from the clutter that repeatedly drives me crazy as I walk around our house. I want them to see financial blessings as something they can use to help the less fortunate instead of a way to build up their collection of easily broken and lost toys.

I want to teach my children that people matter more than businesses, that experiences matter more material possessions, that memories matter more than the trinkets that accompany them. I don't want a desire for stuff to drive our kids' every thought and decision. To be honest, it's always been one of my biggest parenting struggles: how do I teach them to want less stuff when they live in a world where value is defined by how much stuff they have?

More than anything, I want them to see themselves as contributors, not consumers. I don't want them to eschew all personal possessions and live a minimalist lifestyle, but I want them to carefully consider everything they buy and use and how those purchases impact those around them.

I realize that it is a goal that is both privileged and counter-cultural. It's idealistic and often works in opposition to my own desires for prettier, better things. I constantly have to remind myself I need to be an example for my children. If I want them to change the way they see the material world, I need to watch what and how I buy, too.

Part of parenting is to always be learning and doing better. I guess this is just one more way I have to keep growing as well.

Say "I'm Sorry"

IN THE "BEFORE TIMES," when Jeff—who usually works from home—would travel, it would throw off our entire family's rhythm for a couple of days.[1] The kids had to get up earlier so that I could take them to school, I had to get up earlier so that I could get the kids up earlier, and our days were generally just a little bit longer.

It wasn't terrible; it really wasn't. And as our kids got older, it certainly got easier. Gone were the days when I was physically dressing them, and they were generally responsible for themselves once I woke them up. Of course, it didn't always go so smoothly.

One particular example of this happened several years ago, when I discovered that our then-eight-year-old daughter, who just ten minutes earlier had been awake in the bathroom, had decided that she was going back to bed. Thinking that we were ready to go (and we were already running late), I walked into her bedroom to find her in her PJs, back in bed.

My yell *might* have morphed into a horrifying screech as I directed her to get out of bed immediately and get dressed so that we could leave, *now*. I had skipped the typical middle step of reminding the kids one last time that we needed to leave. Instead of announcing thrice, I had only announced twice.

---

1. In the early days of the COVID pandemic, Jeff and I started referring to everything before the pandemic as the "before times." We haven't stopped doing so. It seems like an appropriate reference point for all of the ways our lives changed in the wake of 2020.

It was admittedly far from my proudest mom moment. I was on my third day of temporary single parenting and was dealing with end-of-semester teaching stress. Our daughter should have gotten up and taken responsibility for herself. She knew what she was doing when she went back to bed, and she deserved to be chastised.

She just didn't deserve to see her mom go full banshee on her.

That night, after the dust had settled, we talked about where both of us had gone wrong. She knew what she had done, but I had been wrong too. While my reaction matched my stress levels and irritation at the situation, it certainly didn't match her infraction. I swallowed my pride and apologized for turning into a wicked witch before any of us had really started our day.

It's hard as parents to admit when we have been wrong. It takes humility to admit to our children that we are also human beings who make mistakes. We sometimes worry that it will remove our parental authority and make us doormats to children eager to find any chinks in our armor.

But it is also one of the most important character-building parenting practices we can adopt as imperfect human beings.

My parents were loving and attentive, but the words "I'm sorry" were usually directed towards them instead of coming my direction. I know that a lot of people probably say this, but I was a pretty well-behaved kid and I usually deserved the punishment when I did disobey my parents. And as the eldest of four girls, I was the lab rat. There were stricter rules and expectations put on me as my parents figured out the best way to raise their daughters.

Like most parents, they wanted to raise moral and responsible young women, and when I see how my sisters and I turned out, I think they did a pretty good job. But that doesn't mean they didn't make mistakes along the way, many of which I eventually cataloged as occasional personal slights that were just more reason for my young adult angst.

To be honest, I'm probably still holding onto that mental catalog somewhere.

When we finally became parents, I determined that I was going to be different. Don't we all desire to out-parent our parents? I was going to be more forgiving and less authoritative. I didn't want to be my children's friend but I also didn't want them to see me as an infallible overlord. I desired to find some kind of mythical in-between in my quest for familial harmony.

But I'm human, and I kept making mistakes. I expected too much of our littles and stressed about the small things. When I was pregnant with our son I turned into a hormonal monster that overreacted at every little thing, and our toddler daughter quickly took note of her mommy's unmanageable mood swings. I had no idea how to apologize to a little girl who still lacked the full vocabulary to express her own emotions. I kept praying that she wouldn't remember the mess that her mother became while pregnant with her brother.

Thankfully, Jeff and our daughter survived those nine months, barely.

Once our son was born and our daughter's communication skills continued to grow, I determined I would do better. I would try harder to be patient, I would listen to their concerns and try to help them better express themselves, and I would take the time to focus on them instead of worrying about the outside noise.

And I would *always* personally apologize to them when I screwed up.

In nearly fourteen years of parenting I have learned that it is the hardest and most rewarding vocation I will ever have. Our kids learn from us and I am as encouraged by their love and compassion for the world as I am discouraged by the yells I hear from our daughter when she's angry at her brother, hearing the echo of my own voice when I'm frustrated with one or both of my kids.

Despite my best efforts, there are days that the stress from a day of work, the perpetual mess of my house, or hormonal mood swings push me to overreact to even the little things. Sometimes I overreact for no reason at all. Do my kids push my buttons? Absolutely. Do they disobey or act irresponsibly? Yes, because they are learning boundaries. Do they need discipline when their behavior endangers them or those around them? Yep.

But even in those moments I have to remember to check my response to their behavior. In those moments we have to ask *each other* for forgiveness, them for their behavior and me for the level of my reaction to that behavior. And yeah, sometimes even my own behavior. I want them to learn that anger can be good and justified, but how we express that anger needs to be appropriate to the situation and not be the cause of hurt to those we love. I want them to learn the importance of looking at the whole picture (something I'm constantly learning as well) and considering how their actions and reactions affect those around them. I want them to learn the value of offering grace even when that grace does not appear to be deserved.

I don't want our kids to believe I think I'm always right. I want them to know that adults can be wrong too. I don't want them to grow up believing that being a grown up means never having to own up to their mistakes. I want them to expect that regardless of age, people have to take responsibility when they have wronged others. I don't want them to feel like I'm ignoring their pain just because it sometimes seems so insignificant to me (and admittedly, I'm often not as patient as I should be). I want them to feel that their hurt is real and worth acknowledging so that they can learn how to process that pain in healthy, healing ways.

But just learning how to forgive makes for an incomplete lesson. Forgiveness is an important part of developing relationships, but is only the second half of the equation. They also need to learn to *ask for forgiveness* when they have wronged others, because that is how they *maintain* relationships. As human beings we hurt each other, and whether or not it is intentional, I want them to understand the importance of humility, acknowledging when they have caused pain, and penitently asking for forgiveness. And that is a lesson that can start with me.

I've committed to teaching them that lesson by simply telling them "I'm sorry. Will you forgive me?" It's one of the best parenting decisions this imperfect but forgiven mom has ever made.

Forging Their Own Path

MOST ADULTS WHO SPEND their childhood with parents in prominent positions know that it comes with a combination of perks and unforeseen challenges, some which leave lasting scars. Growing up in a spotlight, no matter how big or small, shapes who we are as adults. And whether right or wrong, it's the others in a person's community that shape the experiences that help form the people we eventually become.

For me, the experience of growing up with a father who took on a variety of roles in our church body was a mixed one, often dependent on the position at the time and my personal proximity to whatever church he was serving. It was also what convinced me that the closest I ever wanted to get to putting my own children into that situation was by my work as a high school teacher, far removed from the actual inner workings of whatever congregation we chose to be a part of.

Let's just say I didn't come out of childhood completely unscathed.

While my dad didn't become a pastor until I was well into my 30s, throughout my adolescence he served in two different congregations as both school principal (for the schools attached to the churches) and in directing the different Biblical educational opportunities for members. I was essentially a pastor's kid before I actually became a pastor's kid once I was an adult. The family business was the church: my mom playing organ many Sundays, my dad leading Bible class and assisting with services, and my sisters and I dutifully going to Sunday School and youth group and leading with our knowledge and expected behavioral example.

During those years I desperately wanted to just be a normal kid without the eyes and ears of members watching my every move. I wanted my peers to see me as a faithful Christian with hopes and dreams and, yes, flaws. I didn't want them to be afraid that I would judge them or tell on them for being teenagers. I wanted them to see me as one of them, not a "goody-two-shoes" they had to behave around. I wanted to be allowed to swear—just once or twice—because I had done something stupid like drop a book on my toe. I didn't want to be "bad"; I just wanted to be seen as normal.

But I also wanted to protect my father from any reason to question his faithfulness to God or ability to do his job. I didn't want people to see my screw-ups as his screw-ups. I was a good kid who didn't want to disappoint my parents by making his job more difficult. I wanted people to judge my father by the job *he* was doing, not by what *I* was doing.

By the time I was attending college with many people who experienced similar upbringings, I concluded that it's no wonder there is a stereotype of pastor's kids, as there are stereotypes for many children with parents in prominent positions. Children don't get to choose their parents, and they don't get to choose their parents' jobs. Rebellion is the one thing they can control.

There's a kind of unrelenting pressure that comes from being a kid with a parent who is in a position of authority. It isn't just that you are expected to act a certain way, it's the other stress that naturally goes with a job in which you can't make everyone happy. Children absorb the criticisms directed towards their parents. It doesn't matter how well parents try to shield their offspring from the uglier parts of their jobs, kids are observant little sponges, well aware of changes in mood and temperament. When they notice hushed conversations, their little detective ears perk up, desperate to understand what is causing Mom and Dad so much worry. They hear what others say about their parents, sometimes from the mouths of their own peers. They are not oblivious to the challenges of the job.

It wasn't until adulthood that I even realized that three presidential children—Chelsea Clinton and Jenna and Barbara Bush—would have been my peers if we had gone to college together. But as I got older and started noticing them going through many of the same life changes as me, I considered what their lives must have been like. What would it have been like to see your parents' marriage challenged in front of the nation? What would it have been like to see your father struggle through the decision to go to war and then attend classes with people who were vocally opposed to that decision? What would it have been like to go to college with all of the challenges of growing up and learning how to be an adult under the careful watch of both the Secret Service and every national news outlet?[1]

It's a miracle they turned out to be the intelligent and balanced women they are today.

Now that I'm a parent, I'm constantly considering how my choices might affect my own children. Honestly, I don't always like what I see. Over the years I've been embarrassed by my kids just being kids in church, convinced that people were watching how a Christian high school teacher's children were behaving. Instead of just letting them roam free at basketball and football games, I've wanted to make sure they were "staying out of trouble." And while our disciplinary issues at school have been minimal, I wondered what second grade teachers were saying about me when my son got in trouble for repeating a profanity on the playground.

It's probably a good thing that we are now living where they will no longer be attending the same school where I teach. At least I've taken that pressure away from them.

I have to consistently remember that my kids have to be allowed to be their own selves. I knew this when I faced the

---

1. This particularly hit home when I read the memoir *Sisters First*, by Jenna Bush Hagar and Barbara Bush. It was then that I realized just how close in age I was to both the Bush twins and Chelsea Clinton. It's amazing how experience and perspective can change over time.

possibility of them attending the same school where I taught.[2] I know this as I watched my children struggle through changes outside of their control because of circumstances around their mom's teaching career. I know this as I pursue my own writing and write about my experiences as a mom and our experiences as a family while I try to allow them to live with some kind of anonymity. I know this as someone who spent most of her adolescence struggling with finding my own identity separate from my dad's position.

And yet I still struggle to give my kids the freedom to make their own choices and decisions. I struggle with the line between guidance and control. I don't want my son to hate soccer because I keep encouraging him to stay on a team just so I can watch him play. I don't want our daughter to decide that she hates theater or choir or writing because I try to direct her to try new things in all of those areas. But we keep telling them to let us know when they don't want to do something anymore, because, in the end, they are the ones who have to keep doing it.

Our children don't get to choose the childhood we've given them. I want to at least give them the freedom to find their way through that childhood.

With a *little* guidance, of course.

---

2. That appears to be a fear of the past. As of right now, my I teach in a different school district than the district in which we live.

Watching Them Play

WE ALWAYS WANTED OUR kids to play sports.

While I clung to my dreams of having a tiny dancer, both our son and daughter left those dreams in the dust by the time they were in elementary school.

When our daughter decided she also wanted to play soccer if her little brother got to play, we quickly joined the tens of thousands of sports parents around the country.

After a failed attempt at basketball when our daughter was in kindergarten, we watched her bloom as a soccer player, and I grew to love watching a sport that had terrified me when I was a child. (Again, I had no desire to have other people kicking at or near my shins.) We expanded our repertoire with basketball and then, eventually, flag football.

We've anxiously watched rain forecasts to determine rain-outs, dragged ourselves out of bed on early Saturday mornings, warmed ourselves with coffee, and baked in the hot Texas sun. A move back to Indiana has meant soccer seasons that start with sunburns and end with hoodies and blankets. I've taken countless photographs with my phone and SLR, proudly posting them to social media and making my kids look more successful on the field than they are in real life. We've supported their desire to be active and play with their friends, paying the necessary funds for sports fees and new shoes and shin guards and dinners consumed on the run while we try to make it from one activity to the next.

But through it all, it has always been just a *part* of our kids' lives, not their entire lives. Travel teams, special leagues, and multiple training camps have never been a part of the discussion.

We've done a couple of special classes for our son over the years, but often discovered that they added little to no value to his experience with the sport, not giving him the break he needs to just figure out life.

My daughter loved playing basketball and soccer, but once we moved to the public junior high school, she quickly discovered an additional love of theater and music, conflicting with a sports career that was most likely going to come to a close once she was in high school. Our son keeps changing his future dreams, and while he currently has stolen my husband's heart with his desire to play for the Big 10, I think we'll just let him be a kid and step up the training if and when he makes up his mind.

After all, our goal has always been kids who love to be active and understand team sports; we never wanted their futures to hinge on an injury-free childhood full of focused training and void of free play.

I like to believe that this balanced approach to athletics makes us reasonable parents. Would we love it if our kids were able to pay for the college education of their choice because they are skilled at a specific sport? Sure, but then I have to ask myself, "at what cost?"

We've watched our friends sacrifice family vacations and hundreds to thousands of dollars to pay for their kids to craft their skills in a single sport. We've watched family members and then our own peers' children suffer from injuries that used to plague adults twice their age. We've watched parents from the sidelines at our own kids' games as they have talked about running from one practice and game to the next, barely slowing down to breathe or even take a moment for themselves.

And then we've looked at each other and mouthed "nope."

A couple of years ago, I spoke to a former student who went to a smaller school on a football scholarship and then eventually decided that the school and the team weren't for him. If he wanted to pursue his new dreams, football was going to have to be a pastime and not remain central to his college career, a decision that he found more freeing than defeating.

Another student confessed that months of social distancing and the shutdown of club volleyball opportunities gave her the chance to try new things, and she started to realize how much she had been missing in the pursuit of scholarship dreams. She wasn't sure that she wanted to keep working at a sport that was keeping her from enjoying just being a teenager.

I've seen students comment on getting burned out of sports they loved because they played too much or it got too competitive and it stopped being fun. I've seen other high school students crushed by career-ending injuries that forced them to rethink their entire futures before they turn eighteen. *And* I've seen students who believe that their experiences in club and high school sports helped to shape them into the young adults they are while giving them opportunities that they never would have had otherwise.

The most well-adjusted of those students are the ones who have the freedom to pursue what they love and make their own decisions concerning their athletic futures.

Maybe it's because we've never seen sports as the end-all-be-all of our kids' futures, but I never cease to be shocked by the parents who lose their minds over a bunch of nine-year-olds learning how to pass or dribble a ball. The arguing with referees who don't have to spend their evenings with crazy parents but still choose to do so. The yelling coaches who forget that they are teachers responsible for not only instructing their charges in the rules and skills of the game, but in how to gracefully deal with disappointments when the game doesn't go their way.

No, I don't like watching my kids lose, and we've seen a lot of that over the years. No, I don't like to see my kids disappointed when they don't get the team spot they want. And no, I didn't like having everything shut down and my kids sitting around doing nothing physical because of arguments that it was too hot to play outside. (And they said this while a pool sat in our Texas backyard begging them to dive in.)

But I also believe there are important lessons in having our kids play while not making it the central focus of their lives or the lives of the entire family. We still need to make space for family vacations, summer jobs, worship, academics, and, yes, general leisure. I believe that one of the reasons we struggled so much as a society when everything initially shut down due to COVID-19 was that we had been running ourselves ragged, and nowhere was this truer than in our overscheduled family lives.

So, yes, we encourage our kids to play. We *should* encourage them to pursue their dreams and set goals. But we also work to avoid allowing them to make that dream and goal the one thing that makes life worth living.

Because selfishly, I really just want to be in the moment enjoying watching my kids do what they love, fully aware that they have our permission to stop when it's no longer fun for them.

Thriving Kids

As both a parent and a teacher, it is a question I have frequently asked myself. How many of my students are in survival mode, and am I partly to blame for their situation? What am I doing for my own kids to help them discover what it truly means to thrive as a person? What roadblocks am I putting in their way, or what am I doing to help them work around the roadblocks that life naturally gives them?

As an American, I often feel like I've been forced to accept survival as the social norm. Even before COVID-19 took over our lives, American society rewarded excessive work with praise and scolded those who chose leisure. We had created a cult of busyness, always working, rarely playing, and turning even the most leisure activities into competitions with friends and strangers (think reading challenges, exercise streaks, and bucket lists). Not that there is anything wrong with that, but when that is all that we are, when we are so busy and focused on the end result that we are just trying to survive until we cross the finish line, we have lost sight of what it means to thrive. And when we allow the same level of pursuit for our children, what are we teaching them about the importance of thriving over surviving?

The mom in me worries that we're not teaching kids to thrive at all.

I've seen it throughout my high school teaching career. I've watched student anxiety grow over inflated GPAs, dependence on test scores, and over-commitment to activity after activity in an effort to boost college applications. Students trip over each other to compete for spots in "top" universities and experience crushing defeat when they don't get into the school of their choice, convinced that their future aspirations have been destroyed by having to "settle" for their second or third choice. Instead of focusing on what they have learned and how that learning has enriched their understanding of the world around them, they pursue the opportunities that will get them the best class rank, often taking advanced courses they aren't interested in or that they struggle with just because a certain grade in those classes will earn them higher points in the GPA scale. And the pressure from home is immense. I once had a student whose mom threatened to pull him out of the school where I taught because he got a B in my dual credit course. I spent forever trying to reassure him that his success was in that he got such a high B in a college course as a high school junior. He had nothing to be ashamed of, and yet the pressure to be perfect was so high that I'm not certain that assurance set in.

Even with my best students, this has led to cheating, depression, extreme test anxiety, and academic burnout before they actually start college and the realistic pursuit of their dream careers. Activities that they loved at the beginning (athletics, music, art) sometimes lose their allure as they realize that the hours they have put into those pursuits have prevented them from enjoying other parts of childhood: family vacations, summer jobs and the independence that extra spending money could give them, dates, dances, and standard leisure time. Adulthood is knocking on their door, and parents and teachers are asking them what they want to do with their futures, and they haven't felt the freedom to just be kids for several years.

What does all of this have to do with me as a mom? Everything.

The experience of watching my students struggle with the conflict between surviving and thriving influenced how I wanted to parent. It started with decisions my husband and I had to make early on. We wanted our kids to have the opportunity to be involved in activities that captured their interest, but we also didn't want to be owned by those activities. How young was too young for dance (a short-lived venture for our daughter) and sports for both of our kids? Were they really ready for basketball and soccer? Were we really ready for the commitment that those activities would take? What about academic bowls and accelerated learning and after school clubs and summer programs? Where would we draw the line, and would we know where the line was *before* we crossed it?

I can't say we've always been successful in managing that balance, but we've tried.

Our kids do well in school, and we expect them to do their best. Throughout their elementary careers, they've known that we expect good grades from them because that is what they are capable of, but what they learn is more important than the final percentage they come home with. We allow them to participate in sports and have stretched our limit with our son, who frequently plays two sports at once. But we refuse to be the parents who give up our family vacations and much needed down time so that our children can be involved all the time in activities that are supposed to be learning and growing experiences, not the determining factor in their future.

Thriving is not achieved through the relentless pursuit of success. It is achieved through time and the freedom to explore. It is achieved through emotional and financial security. It is achieved through support and nurture. We know this, and yet it is still one of the most difficult parenting pursuits for American parents. Some of us face very real roadblocks which need to be removed by changed policy. Some of us are so focused on our missed opportunities that we struggle to see how our desire to make sure our kids also don't miss out might be impacting our kids. Some of us just don't understand the systemic pressures that are weighing down our adolescents, because that pressure just wasn't there when we were kids.

I wish I had the answer. Years of parenting and I still so often feel like I'm grasping at straws with everyone else. The parent in me constantly questions whether my kids are being set up for a thriving future. But I do know that we need to change the lens through which we see our kids' lives and the role we play in it. We need to fight for an environment that allows them to be curious, creative problem solvers. We need to vote for changes to the system so that they and their peers can pursue their dreams and still live healthy and full lives. And we need to give them the space to make those dreams their own.

Motherhood continues to change me as I see problems and seek solutions that will make the world better for the growing young people I have the pleasure of raising to adulthood. And part of that is helping them seek their own thriving and the thriving of others, as long as I can avoid putting up inadvertent roadblocks that get in their way.

Healing

So Many Unknowns

IT HAD BEEN A year of unknowns. No, more like five years of unknowns. Our move to Texas corresponded with a shift in our country that none of us were prepared for. I found myself constantly plagued by increasingly complex questions with each news story that broke across my social media feed.

How could millions of people see the same events with such different interpretations? How could so many of my loved ones support someone who appeared to contradict everything they believed in? Why did people believe so many lies? How could people just ignore the pain of others? Why did I allow myself to get into fights with perfect strangers online? Why did I think that I could change people's minds online? Why did I keep trying, even when it hurt to feel rejected? Why did I feel the need to fix everything?

How could I be the change I wanted to see when so much of what I wanted to say seemed to be grounds for harsh criticism? How could I be the teacher I wanted to be when it felt like I was walking on eggshells? How could I influence without being seen as a troublemaker? Why did it feel like the world was turning upside down? How could I protect my family against an unknown and untested virus? How could I be a good mother when the world was on fire?

What did I believe? How could Jesus feel so close but the institutions I had depended on my entire life feel so far away? How could I hold onto my faith when those whom I trusted seemed to be turning their backs on what was good? What was I supposed to do when the Church felt increasingly distant and uninterested in my concerns about the world my kids were growing up in? What was my role in a Church that didn't want my input?

Who was I, really?

I had no idea that all of those questions were going to come crashing down to crush me in a single night.

Everything Changed

EVERYTHING HURT. MY EYES burned from all of the crying, and my head hurt from my stuffy nose and failed attempts to stop crying when around the kids. The tension in my shoulders worked its way through my entire body, begging for release but not knowing how to do so. When Jeff took the stress ball and worked out the knots from my neck all the way down my back, my muscles turned to jelly, and I didn't know if I would ever be able to move again.

The body keeps the score.

I had spent the previous five years carefully avoiding political landmines as I tried to teach English and history in a political climate that suddenly viewed any criticism of the party in charge as a challenge to both faith and patriotism.

I had spent the last ten months navigating the political and social tightrope of a global pandemic with no sign of it slowing down or stopping.

I went into Lutheran education because I was a Lutheran school kid, the daughter of a Lutheran school educator, and I believed in Lutheran education. I may have graduated from a public high school and believed in the importance of a strong public school system, but I personally wanted to serve in Lutheran schools. I loved the system. I loved the pedagogical freedom of teaching in a private school. I loved being able to tie my faith to our lessons as I also worked to teach my students how to use the lessons of literature and rhetoric and history to better live their faith.

My mission never changed. I hadn't changed. My world had. And apparently my toe had finally bumped against one of those landmines I had worked so hard to avoid.

The specifics don't matter nearly as much as the end result. I started that Friday a teacher with detailed plans for the remainder of the school year. I had a roadmap and personal and professional goals. I had students I loved and colleagues I enjoyed working with. By the time I arrived home, I had no idea if I would ever be a teacher again. I had far more questions than I had answers.

The world to which I had dedicated my life decided that I just didn't fit anymore.

And maybe I didn't, but that didn't make it hurt any less.

Nothing prepares you for starting a day believing one thing about yourself and ending the day not knowing who you are anymore. It would take months before I could start to find answers to the questions that plagued me then and linger now.

All I know is that in a single moment, everything changed. I suddenly lived in the Upside Down, the fictional reversal of Hawkins, Indiana in the Netflix drama, *Stranger Things*. Everything felt strange and wrong. I didn't know whom to trust and what to say. We had talked about returning to church because it started to feel physically safe again, but now I had to wonder if it would be emotionally and spiritually safe. I didn't want to see connected people when I took my kids to school. I didn't want to answer questions to which I didn't have satisfactory answers. Every step felt like a potential landmine.

And I still had to be a wife and mother. While I collapsed in on myself, Jeff held us all together. I didn't know what to even say to the person who knew me better than anyone else. I didn't know myself anymore. What could I possibly say to him? And how could I protect my kids from the unknown when I didn't even know what my next move was going to be on a given day?

It is a lonely space when you lose something overnight, especially something that had been entwined in nearly every aspect of your life. I didn't know where I belonged or if I would ever find a sense of belonging again.

Nearly eighteen months later, I was reading Brené Brown's book *Atlas of the Heart*. She distinguishes between "fitting in" and "belonging." She says:

> We can never truly belong if we are betraying ourselves, our ideals, or our values in the process. That is why it's a mistake to think that belonging is passive and simply about joining or 'going along' with others. It's not. Belonging is a practice that requires us to be vulnerable, get uncomfortable, and learn how to be present with people without sacrificing who we are. When we sacrifice who we are, we not only feel separate from others, but we even feel disconnected from ourselves.[1]

I finally began to see how much of my life had been me attempting to fit into a space instead of actually belonging to the group. I had frequently been on the fringes looking in, saying just the right things to still be considered part of a team but not actually belonging with the team.

In the weeks and months that followed everything blowing up, I started to relax. Over time I realized just how much I had been holding in. I didn't realize how much of myself I had sacrificed until I was forced out of a space I had been trying to squeeze myself into.

On one of many long phone calls, a friend told me that I had spent so much time being Mrs. Styf, maybe now I could finally just be Sarah. I had been splitting myself in two persons for too long, and Sarah was tired of hiding in the shadows. Quoting *Hamilton*, she pointed out, "You wrote your way out." And maybe I had.

But that didn't mean it didn't hurt like hell.

---

1. Brené Brown, *Atlas of the Heart*, p. 159

And even though everything had changed for me, I clung to the idea that things didn't have to change for the rest of the family. I could find a new job. Maybe I wasn't meant to be a teacher anymore. Maybe I could follow my writing dreams. Maybe I could work in an entirely new career.

I didn't want to move. I didn't want to do to our kids what my parents had done to me. I didn't want my problems to become their problems. We could keep our house. They could stay at their school. We could keep our neighbors who had become like a second family to us. We could continue our adventures exploring the American Southwest.

But everything had changed, and that meant the whole family was going to have to change with it. It was the only way that all of us, but especially me, could find a way to heal.

I Got a Tattoo

I HATE PAIN.

I don't know anyone who really LOVES pain, but I actively avoid it. I begged for epidurals with both babies; I dislike the dentist; I put things off when I know they will probably hurt.

So I buried my desire for a tattoo for years, because why would I intentionally cause myself pain for a permanent mark on my body? I played games of "what if" in my head. I considered what I would want tattooed on my body and where I would want said tattoo. I even admired the tattoos of others, but I always came back to the thought, "Nope, I don't want the pain."

But when your head and heart have experienced tremendous pain, when you are trying to heal from deep hurt, sometimes you need to just embrace pain that you choose.

When I told Jeff, he initially balked. His wife hates pain. His wife would have never suggested spending money on something so permanent.

Let's just say he was skeptical that I would go through with it.

But he showed tremendous support despite his misgivings. He researched how to make temporary tattoos so we could practice different types of scripts on different parts of my arm. He looked up different fonts so we could decide which one looked most like me. We transferred ink and I sat with different versions for a few weeks before I finally decided it was time to make it official.

Then I gripped my uncertain husband's hand and sat while I allowed my skin to be permanently marked with the Hebrew words.

Eshet Chayil, a woman of valor. A woman who follows Jesus and understands the cost of standing by her principles. A woman who acknowledges her sinful nature and embraces the forgiveness found in a crucified and risen Christ. A woman who chooses justice and loves a God who asks her to "act justly, love mercy, and walk humbly."[1]

A mark on my arm that will remind me of this every day for the rest of my life.

A few months after I got my tattoo, I finally sat down to read the copy of *A Year of Biblical Womanhood* that had been sitting on my shelf since shortly after Rachel Held Evans' death.

I chose the words for my arm because I had read enough by and about Evans that I knew these were the words I needed as a daily reminder. But as I dove into her year-long journey through Biblical lessons of womanhood, everything I read confirmed my decision to have the words written on my arm. She reminds readers "The Proverbs 31 woman is a star not because of what she does but how she does it—with valor."[2]

On one of many walks that Jeff and I took in the months following our loss, as we discussed options for both me and our family, I suddenly stopped him and said, "You didn't marry a warrior."

He responded, "Sure I did. You just hadn't figured out what you had to fight for yet."

There are other tattoos I could get that commemorate big changes in my life, but this one summarizes where I was in the moment and where I wanted to be headed. I moved on from a transformative winter with a new tattoo emblazoned on my wrist right before the buds started to arrive for an early Texas spring. I had no regrets.

---

1. As I said, Micah 6:8 has become my mantra for a lot of things.

2. Rachel Held Evans, *A Year of Biblical Womanhood*, p. 95

Small Victories, Small Defeats

CAMPING IS SUPPOSED TO be how our family recharges.

That's not to say everything about it is always relaxing or problem-free. Trying to get ready even for a weekend away with two adults, two kids, and two dogs takes planning and preparation, not to mention a couple of hours of packing to make sure everything is in its proper place and all of the equipment is in good shape.

And this particular weekend camping trip added the complication of our daughter's desire to take two friends camping with her for her birthday, making up for the last birthday campout that got canceled along with everything else at the beginning of COVID shutdowns. Adding to the weekend craziness? Our son also had a football game on Friday night, and the closest camping spot that we could find was 120 miles away.

I guess it was a good thing that I wasn't working at the time.

What followed was a full day of traveling up to the campground, parking the camper, returning home so that I could take the girls back up to the site and Jeff could take our son to his football game; they would join us after the game.

We thought *that* was going to be the end of the challenges for the weekend. We would be able to eventually enjoy being in a beautiful spot for thirty-six hours before returning home to the regular busyness that we had allowed to return to our lives, pretending like the previous year of pandemic living had never happened.

If only it had been that easy.

A massive storm cell ripped through East Texas, bringing with it torrential rains that dropped inches of water per hour. Most of Houston was spared the worst of it, and our son's game was never canceled, but I was driving north with three 12-year-old girls, straight into the heart of the storms. While I never lost daylight, I still struggled to see the road for about thirty miles. When we finally arrived, I had to figure out how to feed three growing pre-teens without making my planned dinner because there was no way I could do it in the torrential rain. By the time Jeff arrived with our son, they had missed the worst of the storms, and we could settle in for the night. I was so relieved that I was able to overlook the flickering lights overhead, passing them off as a result of the storms and nothing more.

If only that had been the case.

By noon our indoor lights were so dim that I turned them off. While the girls hiked and played games and our son set out to kill ants (which didn't bother me in the least because, as I've said, fire ants are the spawn of Satan), my husband searched for the cause of our loss of electricity. By mid-afternoon, we had no working interior lights, no working inside refrigerator, and an air conditioner that couldn't turn back on (thank goodness the weather had cleared into blue skies and lower humidity). I tried to stay out of the way and help when I felt like I could be helpful (which wasn't very often), reading while I waited for the call for assistance.

This was not how I wanted our camping weekend to go.

It goes without too much explanation that for our family, 2021 gave 2020 a run for its money. My job loss had turned our family life upside down as I tried to work through what it meant for my career and future and as we worked through what that meant for our family. There were so many emotions to go with it: feelings of failure, inadequacy, uncertainty, and fear of what the immediate future looked like. While I slowly grieved and processed the losses that came with the significant life change, I also found myself constantly looking for small wins. Those wins had been everything from having op-eds published to starting a new part-time job that allowed me to try applying my teaching skills to an entirely different industry.

But none of that changed the fact that the things that had always defined who I was as a professional, a wife, and a mother had been completely turned upside down.

When you're constantly reconstructing a house of cards, it doesn't take much to blow it down. It's not that I wanted to keep working with a deck of cards. I desperately wanted to be building with materials made of stronger stuff. I wanted to be building on firm ground, not shifting sand. And I wanted to stop fearing the next small storm that over a year before I would have been able to dismiss, back when COVID started to change our lives in ways that we hadn't even begun to understand, when quarantines and shutdowns were a novelty that we believed would be over in a month.

I don't know if it is just my friends and family or if it is the pandemic or if it is just the stage of life that we are in, but over the past few years, it feels like the majority of the people in my life are going through significant changes: job loss, divorce, issues with children, health problems, and everything in between. As I've talked to friends from many areas of my life over the last three years, I've felt like so many of us are grasping for a sense of control that always feels inches out of reach. I'm constantly trying to avoid comparing my struggles with those of my loved ones, because for all of us, the challenges are no competition; we all just want to get through them with our heads still above water.

And after a week or so of feeling like the ground underneath me was starting to move a little less, it took a series of challenges in a single weekend to knock me right back down again.

When you're on a constant quest for small victories, small defeats can be crushing.

And that particular weekend was, for me, a lot.

But by the time we got home I was able to see the sunshine. The kids all had a wonderful weekend and we got through nearly forty-eight hours with three pre-teen girls without a significant amount of girl drama. I finished reading a book. Jeff and our son got to go kayaking and the three of us took several bike rides on the flat trails, giving me a chance to try out my mountain bike without any kind of drops that typically have me jumping off the bike before I fall off. When we all got home, Jeff and I drove to get the part to fix our camper, and his tenacious desire to save us at least $1000 in repairs paid off. The electrical problem was fixed.

And while the weekend had taken its emotional and mental toll on me, by the time the kids were in bed, we were both in the right state of mind to join a sibling group phone call to offer comfort to my sister-in-law who was in the middle of her own family struggles. Suddenly, our now-resolved weekend worries seemed pale in comparison.

Sometimes accepting the unexpected means accepting that the current situation is just going to be a constant state of small victories and defeats for the time being. That didn't change the momentary frustrations. That didn't serve as a magic cure for the emotional rollercoaster I couldn't seem to get off of.

But working to accept that reality did give me a place to start healing.

Striving for Perfection

I REALLY DIDN'T NEED a book or a quiz or a podcast to tell me that I'm a perfectionist. I've known that my whole life. My grades had to be perfect. My life had to be neatly planned, and any disruption to that plan sent me spiraling. Home improvement projects that people gush over haunt me because I know where that piece of tile is cracked, I know where the floor was scratched, I know where to find bubbles in the polyurethane finish. When I can't do something well, I just want to quit, freezing into a catatonic state until I figure out how to make it work.

I knew all of that about myself, and then I started digging into the Enneagram.

I know, I know. Not everyone is a fan of personality typing and some think that it's a bunch of voodoo that the rest of us get sucked into because it gives us excuses for who and what we are.

But when the world feels like it is falling apart around you, it really does help to have tools to help us better understand how we specifically function in our world.

I've always sought to be the very best at everything, and that has been especially true in my teaching career. During my first three years of teaching, I was at a very small school where I taught all four grade levels of English. I had to come up with lesson plans and units for four grade levels, grade the homework for four grade levels, and I was still learning how to be a teacher. I would see the innovation of friends at other schools and wonder how in the world they ever came up with those incredible lesson plans. It ate away at my confidence. I knew I was doing my very best, but my best was clearly not good enough.

Then, at my next teaching position, I found myself in a much less stressful classroom situation but was quickly pulled into the theater program. I was a young twenty-something with minimal theater experience leading a program with the expectation of growth. I demanded perfection of myself and my students. I cringed with mistakes that only I knew about. That pursuit of perfection on the stage often led to periods when I let things go in my classroom. Even worse, I frequently let things go with my marriage as I pushed for bigger and better with my students.

Then we moved again and I pursued perfection in grad school because it felt like everything else was falling apart around me. Our fixer-upper was literally falling apart. I was pregnant and *super* hormonal. I was lonely and depressed and A's on papers about Mark Twain and composition theory kept me going. I found a new classroom and pushed my students to the limit, a limit that paid off in the end but took a considerable amount of sacrifice on the road to that perfection.

And after the end of a teaching position at my fourth school, the burden of perfectionism weighed heavily on me.

I'm not the only teacher or mother or person who felt that burden over the years of a global pandemic, when everything we ever knew about how to function in our jobs and lives was turned upside down and suddenly we had to find a whole new way of doing things, all while knowing that the end result was going to be far from perfect.

I'm not the only teacher or mother or person who has felt the crushing disappointment of seeing our friends and neighbors and coworkers not meet our high expectations for behavior and care for others. Ones on the Enneagram see a clear right and wrong and expect other people to do their part. It's just how we see the world, and yet the last few years have challenged that perspective over and over again as we've begged others to do the right thing, not just for themselves but for all of us.

And when the very thing that you've spent years pouring your heart and soul into comes to a sudden end, it takes your breath away.

In *The Road Back to You*, Ian Morgan Cron and Suzanne Stabile write that "unhealthy Ones fixate on small imperfections. These Ones are obsessed with micromanaging what they can. Asserting control over something or someone is their only relief."[1]

For the first several months after losing my job, I found myself doing just that. The loss of a clear routine left me spinning, and checklists overwhelmed me. I've never been good at relaxing, and instead of being still, I found meaningless tasks to keep me busy. I spent time on things that didn't really matter but at the time seemed like small wins. I continued to ignore the things I had always let go of (like the state of my messy house) because the feeling of failure made even cleaning and organizing feel like something I couldn't get right, so why try?

I felt like I had done my best but had still failed. I felt like I had stood up for what was right but it didn't matter. I felt like I had sought justice but I was standing alone.

I had followed my conscience and my life had been turned upside down. My justice-seeking perfectionist kept smacking down my solution-seeking peacemaker wing. I didn't just feel like I was in conflict with my imploding world; I was in conflict with myself.

I've had to grapple with the fact that perfectionism is a lonely space. A space where you know you should ask for help, where you shouldn't go it alone, but something keeps telling you that to ask for help is to accept failure.

Throughout my life, my perfectionism has been one of my greatest assets and my biggest enemy. It has made me the person that I am—preparing me for the blows but making those blows so much harder to take. The reality is that at some point, the perfectionist is going to crack under the pressure of trying to be what everyone else expects of them. And when they crack, they

---

1. Ian Morgan Cron and Suzanne Stabile, *The Road Back to You*, p. 91

aren't undergoing a complete transformation; they are becoming a more authentic version of the person that they've always been.

I've slowly been able to once again embrace a healthy state of perfectionism, one which forgives people for the ways they have failed me and others, one that holds onto principles but is patient with stragglers as we slowly make the world a better place. I am far from perfect at this, however. I struggle to find the balance between insisting that people do what is right and allowing them to find the way on their own. I want the changes to happen in my own time, on my terms, which takes me back to the unhealthiest parts of being a perfectionist.

Some days, I'm just trying to maintain enough self-awareness to get me from one task to the next. Other days I find just enough grace for me and for others.

And maybe someday I'll find the capacity to focus on my messy kitchen table and office desk.

Light in the Darkness

OUR FAMILY HAS TAKEN a lot of cave tours. During every tour we have ever taken, there is a moment when the tour guide turns off all the lights, asking those on the tour to also keep their cell phones put away and avoid looking at their watches to avoid ambient light. The goal is to throw the entire group into absolute darkness.

It is thick and disorienting. You can't see your hand in front of your face. Individuals who have found themselves lost in a cave without any kind of artificial light have been known to lose their minds within forty-eight hours. Those who are lost in caves for more than a couple of weeks have their sleep patterns severely disrupted and have trouble with their eyesight. The sudden loss of all light of any kind disrupts the entire human biological system and can cause permanent psychological and physical damage in the most extreme cases.

After a few minutes, the tour guides turn the dim and scattered lights back on. What had moments before been merely mood lighting and a way to prevent visitors from losing the path is suddenly so much more.

When you're lost in a cave, even a flickering light can be the difference between life and death.

Ever since January 2020, I have chosen a word for every year. In preparation for 2021, I chose the word "light."

My goals for the year were noble. I wrote on Instagram, "I want to shine light on the good things happening all around us. I want to look optimistically to the future. I want to show others that Jesus is good even when his followers often aren't. I want to be the change that I want to see in the world."

I had high hopes. After all, the year before I had selected "hope" as my word for 2020, and look how that went. A novel virus turned our lives upside down. Civil unrest followed the undeniable evidence that our country still had far too much work to do to heal our racial wounds. The election had been the most emotionally and spiritually exhausting one of most of our lives, testing bonds of friendships and family ties.

But as 2020 came to a close, I was still holding onto hope.

Looking back, it feels naive, foolish, and entirely too optimistic for the time we were—and still are—living in. True, there were a lot of reasons for hope. A new administration appeared poised to take on many of the challenges that had reared their ugly head during the course of 2020. We were in the early stages of vaccine distribution and it looked like we could possibly be out of the pandemic sooner than later. People were having open and honest conversations about the problems that faced our country, and many appeared to be ready to take them head-on. As an educator, I was watching people have real conversations about what we had learned in the last year about our education system, and there seemed to be a willingness for reform. And a new year was around the horizon. 2021 had to be better, didn't it?

When I look at end-of-2020 Sarah, I don't know whether to laugh or cry at her naivete.

I chose the word "light" for 2021 to be a metaphor for how I wanted to live my life moving forward. Already hopelessly optimistic by nature, I wanted to renew my optimism about the future and all the possibilities of what we could be individually and as a nation. I had spent the previous year becoming increasingly vocal about politics in my personal life because I wanted to be a light to my former students and those around me to show them that, as Christians, there was a better way for us to interact with our political system and with each other. I wanted to show them that loving our neighbors and seeing our communities as interdependent made us stronger, not weaker.

But when our family's life fell apart just weeks into 2021, I found that it was hard to *be* light when *you personally can't see the light*. When you're falling down into a dark abyss with nothing to grab onto, you can't help anyone else. You can't offer hope because you need someone to offer it to you. You can't make decisions about even the simplest things because your agency has been stripped from you. You question everything you are and believe in because someone else has decided that those things have no value. You temporarily lose your voice because you were told that your voice is not wanted.

Suddenly, all you need is for someone else to hold the light *for* you because all forms of light burn your eyes and skin. Light is supposed to offer security and a way out, but, instead, it just hurts.

Slowly, the light came back. It came back in the form of friends around the country who constantly checked in to offer listening ears and good advice. It came back in the form of family that kept reminding us that we were loved and wanted and that we could always come home. It came back in my renewed faith in a God that wouldn't fail me even when the institutions that claimed to preach His Word did.

I had no way of knowing that choosing "light" for my word of the year would be ironic. I could not have predicted anything that happened to us in 2021, including a move back to Indianapolis.

But as I prepared to exit 2021, I was realizing that maybe my choice of the word "light" was really less about what *I* was going to do during the year and more about what God was going to do *for* me through the light of others. In a year that was completely unexpected, I could finally see the faint glimmer of light at the end of the dark tunnel. It wasn't fading; it was growing.

And I found that it would light the way to healing, as well.

Handle with Care

I sat on the top stair of our house and sobbed in the empty hallway.

That morning I had spent most of a church service stubbornly wiping away tears that refused to stop falling. Before church, I had completed a morning social media tour with post after post of friends announcing their middle schooler's confirmation and congratulating them on their affirmation of faith.

My daughter was supposed to be one of them. My daughter was supposed to have spent the previous year learning and studying and growing with her best friends under the guidance of a pastor whom she had spent several years getting to know and a spiritual leader whom I trusted with my daughter's walk with God.

Instead, we were 1000 miles away, still feeling the limbo of unplanned changes that kept us second-guessing.

And what caused the dam to burst?

Just thirty minutes before, when we arrived at the football fields for our son's flag football game, he panicked and announced that he didn't have his mouthguard. I immediately turned around and headed home and after looking at my mess of a house and a frantic search through that mess, I learned on a quick phone call to my husband that a mouthguard had been found and everything was okay and I could just come back.

I. Fell. Apart.

In that moment I was a fragile human being caring for fragile human beings just trying to glue the broken pieces back together.

In some places, the superglue was holding, thanks to the love and support of friends and family. In other places, the pieces were still being held together with clear Scotch tape, the cracks showing through and the adhesive barely holding on.

I knew I was not alone.

Seven years of political turmoil and three years of living through a global pandemic that brought countries and communities to their knees left a lot of us feeling depleted. Far too many of us were and still are holding onto far too much: too much grief, too much hurt, too much fear, too much loneliness.

There are still days that I wish I could walk around with a "Handle with Care" sign. There are still days that I wish I could attach a similar sign to my children, to warn people that I need them to know that my kids are more fragile than they might appear. And yet, in an individualistic culture that still elevates personal strength over healthy interdependence, asking for such a sign feels like I'm asking too much.

To "handle with care" does not mean coddling or focusing on the bright side. Instead, it means acknowledging a person's struggle and refusing to intentionally add on to that struggle. It's recognizing that someone's reaction to your comment or question might not be because of the question but because of everything that lies under the surface of that question. It's admitting that you may have unintentionally hurt someone with your words and actions, and you are asking for forgiveness and attempting to heal the relationship.

It's operating under the philosophy of "do no harm" because that may be the best way you can show love to your neighbor.

I can't even begin to count the number of times in the last two years I've swallowed an "eff you" in response to another person's less-than-care-driven comments or flippant response to my concerns or expressed struggles. Because when someone is hurting, they don't need half-hearted platitudes; they need someone to listen without judgment. And yeah, sometimes they also need someone to sit with them and agree, "that's bullshit," even if they don't fully agree.

Because sometimes it won't go away. Sometimes the outcome can't be changed. Sometimes it can't be fixed.

We need people who will be honest with us. And, yes, I suck at this. I'm a fixer. I'm a peacemaker. I don't want to rock the boat.

I spent years walking on eggshells, trying to avoid politically motivated landmines. I kept my mouth shut when my heart was telling me to speak up. I sometimes compromised my values under the mistaken belief that it was for some kind of greater good. I did all of this only to have it all eventually blow up in my face.

I was, and am still, tired.

I'm tired of holding it all together to make others feel better. I'm tired of acting like I can keep handling even the *little* disruptions that get tossed my way, because my ability to deal depends on a given moment on a given day. I'm tired of my perfectionist nature being at war with my desire to be a peacemaker, because all I really want is justice.

I needed people to just deal with the fact that I was a little fragile. I spent more than a year seeking bubble-wrapped situations because I just didn't know how to safely exist in a world that seems intent on caring for self instead of others.

And as I continued to struggle through all of the emotions that entails, I kept praying for healing and peace and something better around the corner, because that is all I really had the strength to do.

A Phoenix

It had been one year since our lives were turned upside down.

One year since sobs started escaping my body without warning. One year since my body became a ball of tension that hurt to move. One year since the panic attacks and inability to make even the smallest decisions plagued my daily life. One year since I had to re-learn how to communicate with my family, especially my husband, as we tried to find a way forward.

One year since the life I thought we would always have was swept away in an instant.

As I looked back on the emotions of that year, I couldn't help but be overwhelmed by the realization that I had spent the vast majority of the twelve months holding onto far too many feelings at one time.

The fear of telling my children that their life was changing, certain that they would blame me for everything that was happening to them. This was especially true as our son asked us "does this mean we will have to move?" and five months later the answer would be yes.

The embarrassment as I questioned my worth as not just a teacher, but as a human being and child of God.

The pain of feeling betrayed by the silence of people who I thought were friends.

The loneliness of being isolated from what I thought was my community and the painful discovery that I didn't really belong.

The righteous anger of believing that I had followed my heart and God's desire and the questions I had about others as I asked God why.

The grief of loss, so much loss, not just for me but for my entire family.

In Greek mythology, the phoenix is an immortal bird that goes through the cycle of birth, life, death, and rebirth. In the Harry Potter series, Fawkes, Dumbledore's phoenix, shocks Harry as he dies in a burst of flames and is reborn as a baby bird. This phoenix also has special powers of healing through its tears, saving Harry and his friends on more than one occasion.

And so the phoenix can be a metaphor for the rollercoaster of life.

By June of 2021, my internal phoenix had completely burned to ashes. The baby bird that timidly poked up its little beak was unsure of how to take flight, but it knew it had to start over.

We made the most impulsive decision of our marriage and decided it was time to go "home." While we could still say that Texas had been good to us in six years and given us so much, in the end, we had lost too much and we needed to be where we felt we really belonged.

We survived the most miserable vacation of our marriage and yet were still planning what we wanted to do for the next summer vacation.

We bought a house, sight unseen, which in the last eighteen months has become a hub of multiple family gatherings as our kids become reacquainted with cousins and we renew friendships.

I learned to say no to a situation that was harming me and my family and say yes to something better when I made the unprecedented decision to change schools in the middle of a semester.

We returned to Michigan for the first time in five years, first for a football game that caused our kids to fall in love with one of our favorite northern cities, then at Christmas when we finally got to see "our" lake again after far too long, then again for a quick summer trip that included time with grandparents, swimming in our favorite lake, and a stop at Kilwin's for ice cream.

And through it all, I learned that, even when I felt weakest, I am stronger than I thought I was.

The worst year of my life was, in many ways, the start of something we didn't know we needed.

Because two things can be true at the same time.

I can still see my children's grief and ache for them while knowing that, in the long run, the decisions *we* made in the wake of disaster are what is best for them.

I can still grieve the loss of friendships while remaining forever thankful for the ones who stuck by my side and walked with me along the way.

I can be still be hurting and nursing my wounds while fully recognizing that those wounds brought me to a better place.

I can still be in the midst of spiritual trauma and have a stronger faith in the One who doesn't forget His promises.

I can still feel called to the vocation of teaching without it defining everything that I am and allowing it to decide how I live my life.

And the lessons keep coming.

I spent a year in the wilderness, watching the old me burn to ashes so that I could be reborn into something that is still me, but better.

But the wilderness doesn't have to be a place of desolation, it can be a place of growth that often remains unseen until we are safely back at home.

And now the phoenix is once again learning to take flight, ready to leave the wilderness for something better than was there before. As scary as that unknown is, I'm ready to see where it will fly next.

One Year Later

SOCIAL MEDIA APPS HAVE a funny way of bringing back memories and helping you remember anniversaries. A year after our move to Indianapolis, I got a lot of photo memories related to our move to Texas seven years before. It was a move that we were so excited for because it was something new and different and took us away from the Midwest, which had been our home for most of our lives.

For most of those six years, our new lives as Texans was a true adventure. We saw things we never thought we would see. We explored the diversity of our new home state, traveled to the western United States, and started a Thanksgiving camping tradition. It was a good life, until it wasn't.

So we returned to the Circle City where we had family, remaining friendships, and we could pick up the pieces and put ourselves back together with the help of those who had loved and known us best.

The first year back in Indianapolis was far from perfect. I started one teaching job that I was really excited about only to discover that the position was so stressful that I spent Sunday nights yelling at my family for absolutely no reason. For the first time ever, I willingly left a position during the school year (something teachers are trained to *never* do because it's not in the "best interest of the students") and started at a new school with a new department where I continue to feel the most at home that I've felt in years. I know that I have challenges ahead of me as education and expectations keep changing, but in my second year I was in the same building, in the same classroom, and with mostly the same colleagues as I ended with the last school year. I was more excited than apprehensive as I started my second year.

We faced significant challenges on the parenting front, as we tried to manage our own moving transition and two new jobs for me while also helping our kids make the rocky transition in the middle of adolescence. For the first several months we faced a lot of tears, yelling, proclamations about how we had ruined their lives, and uncertainty about the future. We made one important decision after another as we tried to give them the support they needed and often felt like we were failing. And because sometimes we need big changes, the next school year we put our daughter in public schools for the first time ever in hopes that a big change would help her find her place and her people before starting high school. For the first time since our kids were in daycare or pre-school, they were in different schools on different campuses. It was a big change for all of us, but also a good one.

Since we've moved back, we've visited old haunts and discovered new possibilities. We remembered how much we love fall, and I grudgingly admitted that I missed the snow. We finally made it back to Michigan and made one very quick summer trip on a perfect beach weekend so we could enjoy the lake at her very best. Even better, an exhausting trip to Houston so the kids could see friends did not break me like I feared that it would. Instead, it reminded me of the friendships and experiences and good that came from our six years there while making it abundantly clear that we had made the right decision to move. It will always be a part of us, and I'm honestly okay with that. Our lives are richer for the good we experienced while we lived there, and for that I am thankful.

One year after our life-changing move, I can honestly say that I like the Sarah that is emerging. She has scars that will never completely heal, but they are slowly fading. She still struggles with what was lost but is celebrating what has been gained as well. She is tougher and braver than she ever thought possible.

And while there is a lot that she still wishes she could change, she hasn't given up believing that change is possible.

Honestly, it's been better than I could have hoped for as we continue to move forward.

A Work-in-Progress

My blogs, *Accepting the Unexpected Journey* and *On the Journey*, started as a way for me to talk about how things kept changing for our family, but the reality is that it was about so much more. Our family survived two more moves, a hurricane and other severe weather events, travels all over the South, and a devastating job loss and the many changes that went with it.

In the background, we also learned to navigate a world that was changing faster than we could comprehend. We watched social media connect us to our loved ones and then bring out the ugliest sides of those same loved ones and ourselves. We watched a world brought to its knees by a global pandemic that changed everything we thought we knew about the institutions keeping our families together and learned what it really meant to care for our neighbor. And we watched our government get brought to its knees and nearly destroyed by lies and violence spread by the very social media that had promised to unite us when we first logged into our shiny new accounts.

And through it all, I just kept observing and writing and reflecting from the sidelines.

Reading through nearly seven years of blog posts helped me see both the evolution of the woman I am today and the revelation that the woman I am today has always been there. I truly believe that I haven't changed. As I said when I entered my forties, I just became a more authentic version of myself.

As with all journeys, the trip has been far from linear. I can see where I walked in circles as I tried to navigate my way out. I can see the hills and the valleys. I can see the mountain peaks of joy and fulfillment and the gullies of deep despair. I can see where I made huge mistakes and where the hard decisions were the right ones.

But most importantly, I can see who I am right now, and I like what I see.

I'm willing to love and be loved, but I want to be loved for who I am, not who someone else wants me to be. I want to open my heart to new people and experiences, but I'm having to learn how to trust again. I have strong opinions and feel like I have the life experience to share them now, but I also recognize that there is so much that I still don't know, and I'm open to learning more. I'm learning to roll with the punches, even on the days that minor changes send me into a spiral.

And maybe someday I'll truly learn what it means to *embrace* all the unexpected moments in the journey of life.

Notes

Acknowledgments

THERE ARE SO MANY people whom I need to thank for encouraging me along this journey to writing this book.

Thank you to all of those who have read my blogs over the years, sticking with me as I wrote my way through learning and discovery. The faithful few who have read nearly every word I've written over the last ten years are the ones who convinced me that I still had something worth saying and there were people who would read it. I probably would have given up the writing dream if you hadn't kept encouraging me along the way.

Thank you to Rachel Hill and Alicia Drier, my consistent "first" readers. Rachel, you have been reading my writing since we were naive college students with big dreams about the future. To say we aren't where we thought we would be twenty years ago would be an understatement, but I'm thankful our friendship has survived moves, family, and career changes. Thank you for believing in me enough to take the beautiful headshots I've been using for the last two years. Someday I hope to be reading your book as well. Alicia, from teaching colleague to podcasting partner, I have always been able to count on you to encourage me to be better as a teacher and a writer. Iron sharpens iron, and that has been true of our friendship and partnership. This book wouldn't be what it is without your feedback and encouragement.

To the rest of my beta team—Caitlin May Dinger, Bethany Nummela-Hanel, Craig Harmann, Jenny Owens-Cripe, Lauren Tarbet, Anna Maschke, and April Campbell—thank you for taking the time to edit, suggest, and rearrange this book into what it is now. You were able to see gaps where I couldn't and encouraged me to go further when fear held me back. Thank you for volunteering your time to read and respond over the two months I worked to refine this piece. I pray that your efforts will not be in vain.

Thank you to Karen Carson Bennett for your editing work and to Matt Holman for your cover design. Karen, your friendship is a beautiful example of what can happen when you keep in touch with those who were just friendly acquaintances. Our friendships highlights all of the ways the internet still connects us instead of just dividing us. Matt, who knew that when we were college freshmen that our friendship would still be strong enough for me to trust you with designing the cover for my first book? Thank you for your friendship through so many stages of our lives, your support when life seemed to be falling apart around us, and for forgiving us for picking up and leaving Houston while you were still on your summer vacation.

To L and E, thank you for all of the lessons you have taught me about life and love over the last fourteen years. You didn't choose the challenges we have faced as a family, but I hope that someday you will be able to see just how much your dad and I loved you through the decisions we made that turned your lives upside down. God loves you and so do we. I can't imagine my life without being your mom.

Finally, thank you Jeff. This book would never have happened if it weren't for you. Thank you for every way you have supported me over the last 25+ years together. Thank you for tolerating the days when I close the office door to frantically type to meet deadlines, both those set by editors paying me a small stipend and those arbitrary deadlines I set for myself for no money at all. Thank you for giving me the space to try new things. Thank you for not stopping me from publicly writing about our life together. But most importantly, thank you for sticking with me through all of the changes that life has thrown our way. There is no perfect person, but we are perfect for each other. I'm glad that God laughed at my adolescent plans for the future, because I love our life together. The highs and lows, the laughter and tears, the ways we have grown towards each other. I love you, and I'm so glad I said yes to a Fourth of July date with a boy who was never supposed to become my husband.

Thank you, reader, for embracing the journey with me. We're all in this together, because, in the end, together is all we have.[1]

---

1. One of my favorite podcasters, Sarah Steward Holland of *Pantsuit Politics*, has taken to regularly saying this when talking about hard things. I cannot think of a better way to describe the necessity of community in the journey of life.

Works Mentioned

Brown, Brené. *Atlas of the Heart: Mapping Meaningful Connection and the Language of Human Experience*. Random House Publishing Group, 2021.

Cain, Susan. *Quiet: The Power of Introverts in a World That Can't Stop Talking*. Crown, 2013.

Cron, Ian Morgan, and Suzanne Stabile. *The Road Back to You: An Enneagram Journey to Self-Discovery*. InterVarsity Press, 2016.

Evans, Rachel Held. *A Year of Biblical Womanhood: How a Liberated Woman Found Herself Sitting on Her Roof, Covering Her Head, and Calling Her Husband "Master"*. Thomas Nelson, 2012.

Hager, Jenna Bush, and Barbara Pierce Bush. *Sisters First: Stories from Our Wild and Wonderful Life*. Grand Central Publishing, 2017.

Hatmaker, Jen. *Fierce, Free, and Full of Fire: The Guide to Being Glorious You*. Thomas Nelson Incorporated, 2020.

Hatmaker, Jen. *For the Love Podcast*, https://jenhatmaker.com/podcast/. Accessed 25 December 2022.

Miner, Julianna W. "The Sweet Spot of Parenthood Exists, I'm in It Right Now." *Scary Mommy*, 26 August 2019, https://www.scarymommy.com/the-sweet-spot. Accessed 12 October 2022.

Niequist, Shauna. *I Guess I Haven't Learned That Yet: Discovering New Ways of Living When the Old Ways Stop Working*. Zondervan, 2022.

Rowling, J. K. *Harry Potter and the Order of the Phoenix*. Scholastic Incorporated, 2018.

About the author

Sarah Styf lives just outside of Indianapolis with her husband, two children, two dogs, and, now, two axolotls. When she isn't teaching high school English, she enjoys camping with her family, running and biking for recreation, reading, and writing. You can subscribe to her blog and newsletter at sarahstyf.substack.com or follow @sarah.styf on Instagram.